Cambridge English Readers
....

Level 5

Series editor: Philip Prowse

All I Want

Margaret Johnson

CAMBRIDGE
UNIVERSITY PRESS

CAMBRIDGE
UNIVERSITY PRESS

University Printing House, Cambridge CB2 8BS, United Kingdom

Cambridge University Press is part of the University of Cambridge.

It furthers the University's mission by disseminating knowledge in the pursuit of
education, learning and research at the highest international levels of excellence.

www.cambridge.org
Information on this title: www.cambridge.org/9780521794541

© Cambridge University Press 2000

First published 2000
Reprinted 2015

Printed in the United Kingdom by Hobbs the Printers Ltd

A catalogue record for this publication is available from the British Library

ISBN 978-0-521-79454-1 Paperback

Contents

Characters

Alex Faye: personal assistant to Brad Courtney, at the Courtney Art Gallery, Brighton.
Brad Courtney: owner of the Courtney Art Gallery.
Barry: Alex Faye's boyfriend.
Diana: Alex Faye's close friend.
Tania Stevenson: Brad Courtney's girlfriend.
Willow (Betty): Alex Faye's mother.
Christopher: Brad Courtney's nephew.

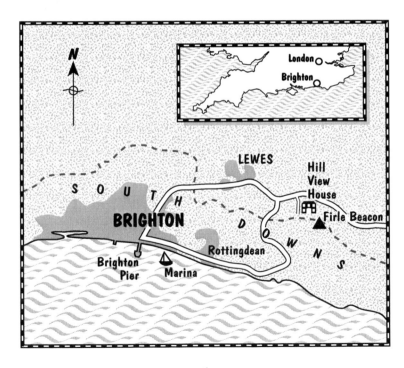

Chapter 1   *A bad start to a birthday*

I wake up feeling sick. This is partly because I drank so much wine with my friends last night, but mostly because today's my thirtieth birthday.

Thirty years old. I can't believe it. I just can't believe it. How can I be thirty?

OK, OK. I know thirty isn't exactly old, but it's a lot older than twenty-nine, believe me. You see, I had a long list of things I wanted to do before I was thirty. Actually, now I've got two lists, my original list and a new one, because three weeks ago my life changed forever. But I'll tell you about that in a moment. Here are the lists:

List One
1. Travel around the world.
2. Write a bestselling book.
3. Buy a house or a flat, preferably with a garden and a sea view.
4. Give up smoking.
5. Give up headaches due to drinking too much.
6. Give up problem boyfriends.
7. Go skiing this Christmas instead of visiting my family.

List Two
1. Have a conversation with Brad Courtney lasting longer than five minutes and without my knees shaking.

2. Get through a whole day at work without annoying Brad Courtney with my careless mistakes.
3. Tell my boyfriend Barry I do not want to go out with him any more.
4. Tell Brad Courtney I love him.
5. Get married to Brad Courtney.
6. Go skiing this Christmas with Brad Courtney.
7. Have Brad Courtney's children, preferably a girl and a boy, both with his beautiful dark eyes.

By now I think you will have guessed that three weeks ago I met Brad Courtney and fell madly in love with him. You might also have guessed that he's not in love with me.

Yet.

I work for Brad, or at least I do while his assistant, June Weatherby, is in hospital. June broke her leg when she fell off a horse. I wouldn't want you to think I'm happy that she's lying in pain in her bed at the hospital, because I'm not, of course. However, I am very happy that her accident has given me the chance to work for Brad. If June's horse had been a calm sort of horse instead of a wild one called Flame, then I'd never have met Brad and I'd never have fallen in love with him.

I work for a temp agency, you see. They find temporary staff for people like Brad. I've never had a job for longer than two months, and most of them are only for two or three weeks, sometimes even one week. I like the variety, the different people and the different work. Or at least I used to. Now I think I'd be happy to stay at the Courtney Art Gallery forever.

Brad, oh Brad. I know it must be almost time to get up,

but as it's my birthday I'm allowing myself to stay in bed for a little longer to dream about him. Brad's so handsome, so clever, so important. He's also so attached to his perfect girlfriend, Tania. Life just isn't fair.

After a while I carefully open my eyes and look at the clock. Five past ten. *Five past ten!* I'm an hour late!

I jump out of bed and quickly get dressed. Brad Courtney might be handsome, clever and important, but he also has a habit of being cross. I'm in serious trouble.

Again.

In the three weeks I've been working at the art gallery, I've already been late four times. And how will I ever marry Brad and have his children if he asks me to leave my job and I never see him again?

'Shoes, shoes!' I cry as I run from the bedroom, trying to brush my hair and button up my blouse at the same time, almost tripping over as I go. The living room's untidy with the remains of the small party I held last night. There are wine glasses, wine bottles, chocolate papers . . . but no shoes.

'Think, Alex, think!' I tell myself, holding my head. Then I see one shoe underneath the sofa. *One* shoe. Where's the other one?

'Oh hell!' I go back into the bedroom with one shoe on and eventually find the other one hiding under the bed. I quickly put it on and run to the front door. There's a pile of birthday cards on the doormat and I pick them up and run to catch the bus.

I often walk to work. It takes about twenty minutes or so, but it's a nice walk through the park and then along the seafront into the centre of Brighton. I like it at all times of the year. Last winter there was even snow on the beach! But this morning there's no time for a pleasant walk, and luckily for me there's a bus coming down the hill. I put my hand out to stop it.

'Where are you going, love?' The bus driver smiles at me. So do the other passengers. Either everyone's being very friendly, or . . . I look down at my clothes and realise my coat's buttoned up wrongly: on one side it's dragging on the floor and on the other side it's lifted up to my knees. I smile at everybody, pretending to be perfectly happy to wear my coat like that, and take a seat right at the back of the bus. Then I sigh and close my eyes. What a way to start a birthday: tired, ill, embarrassed and late for work. Still, at least I've been sent plenty of birthday cards. Unless they're all Christmas cards and everybody's forgotten my birthday!

The first one I open is a birthday card from my brother, Rob. 'I can't think of you as being thirty,' it says on the front. And inside is, 'without dying of laughter.' There's a badge attached to the front. 'Thirty today!' it says. Well, I won't be wearing that.

The card from Mum and Dad isn't much better. There's a note inside written in Mum's untidy handwriting. 'Thirty years old! I can't believe so much time has passed. It almost makes me feel old.' Fantastic.

I search the pile of envelopes to find a card that might be a bit more cheerful and recognise the handwriting of my friend Susan. 'Beauty Queen,' it says on the front of the card. That's better, even if it isn't true. I suppose I'm almost pretty, but I'm certainly not beautiful. Especially when I've got a headache and I haven't had time to put any make-up on.

I open the card. 'Wishing you all you wish for yourself in the year ahead,' Susan has written.

Frowning, I put the cards back into my bag. My friends have very clear ideas about what they want from life. Susan wants to be an office manager, Diana wants to save the world and Kerry wants to be a famous dancer. They all care about their work a lot. Whereas I just do a little of this and a little of that without ever getting very far.

Perhaps it's time to change all that. Perhaps I should make up my mind to do the things on both my lists in the year ahead. Yes, why not? After all, I might not be interested in being an office manager or a dancer, but I *am* interested in Brad Courtney. Very interested. OK, so I've only known him for three weeks, but what difference does that make? I fell in love with him at first sight, at the job interview.

Yes. This time next year I'll be married. To Brad. I'll also be finishing off my bestselling book before going on a skiing holiday over Christmas. With Brad. And while we're on holiday, we'll try to make a baby. No, two babies: twins. A son and daughter. A little Brad and a little Bradette.

'Weren't you getting off here, love?' the bus driver calls out to me kindly, and I get quickly to my feet.

'Oh, yes! Yes, thank you.' How can I have been so busy with my daydreams that I almost travelled past my bus stop? Aren't I late enough already?

'Have a good day, love,' the driver says just before the bus doors close, and looking back I see he's laughing.

The Courtney Art Gallery is in Ship Street, just off the seafront. When I get there it's almost half past ten. I stop a few metres away and take a few deep breaths, then I walk up to the door. But the door won't open. The gallery's locked. Amazed, I stand there and look through the window. The gallery is never closed on Monday mornings. Where's Brad?

I stand there worrying for a while, and then suddenly I see a familiar face next to mine in the glass.

'Brad!' I turn, my face going red as it often does when I'm near him. Oh, how I wish it didn't! But he's so attractive and I like him so much it makes me feel nervous. And when I feel nervous I either can't think of anything to say or I say the wrong thing and end up looking stupid. Today though, I'm too worried about Brad to think about myself. He looks tired and ill, and his face is very pale.

'I'm so sorry, Alex,' he is saying. 'You've been here since nine o'clock.'

'Er . . .' I say, wondering whether I should explain about being late myself.

'It was very good of you to wait,' he continues, and I shut up. Well, it won't harm anyone if he thinks I've been waiting outside the gallery for one and a half hours, will it? And he'll never know I was late.

'Come on,' he says, 'I'll buy you a coffee to apologise.'

'Er, thanks,' I say, but he's already walking quickly away.

I run after him, wondering whether I should ask what has happened, or whether I should just wait until he tells me. But what if he doesn't tell me? I'll die of curiosity.

'Er . . .' I say, running after him along the street, 'is . . . everything all right?'

'No,' he answers, walking quickly on.

'Oh,' I say, and because I can't think of anything else to

say after that, I remain quiet until we're seated at a table in the Sea View Café at the end of the street.

We order coffee and, when it arrives, Brad drinks his silently for a while before looking at me across the table.

'Alex,' he says seriously, 'I have a very important question to ask you.'

I swallow, feeling nervous again. He's going to ask me out to dinner. He is. Brad Courtney's going to ask me out on a date! Perhaps he knows it's my birthday!

'Y-yes?' I say in a shaking voice, and he looks at me with his beautiful dark eyes.

'Why are you wearing one black shoe and one white shoe?' he asks.

'What?' I say. For a long moment I don't understand him, and then he begins to laugh. Loudly. I look nervously down at my feet and see that it's true. On my left foot I'm wearing a black shoe, and on my right foot I'm wearing a white shoe. I remember the laughter of the bus driver and the smiles of the other passengers and I understand suddenly why they were so amused.

'Oh, no,' I groan, putting down my coffee cup. I close my eyes, covering my face with my hands. Brad's still laughing, and for a horrible moment I imagine myself at our wedding. There I am at the church in a white wedding dress. I'm walking with my father towards Brad, and all the guests are turning to look at me. Brad turns to look at me too, smiling. Then suddenly he starts to laugh, exactly as he's laughing now. I look down at my feet. There they are, at the bottom of my beautiful wedding dress, one in a white shoe and the other in a black shoe. And suddenly all the guests are laughing – even the priest's laughing – and my face is turning bright red.

'Oh, that's so funny,' Brad's saying now. 'Thank you, Alex, you've quite cheered me up.'

'All right,' I say, my face really red now.

'Is it the latest fashion?' he asks. 'If I go back outside will I see other people wearing different coloured shoes? One red shoe and one brown shoe perhaps? Or what about one green and one blue?' He begins to laugh again and I sit and look at him. I try to make myself hate him, but I can't do it.

'Why were you late this morning?' I ask, and immediately he stops laughing and drinks some more of his coffee.

Before he can answer, the café door opens, bringing in both a man and the wind straight from the sea. I recognise the man. It's Arthur Grant, one of the gallery artists. He paints landscapes and is one of Brad's most successful clients. This is probably one of the reasons why Brad's always so friendly towards him.

'Arthur!' Brad's calling out to him, 'Good to see you! Let me buy you a coffee!'

Arthur Grant is never a happy man, but today he looks angry as well as unhappy. 'Where have you been?' he demands. 'I've been trying to get into the gallery ever since nine o'clock this morning! There was nobody there!'

Brad looks at me across the table. My face goes red again.

'I'm so sorry, Arthur,' Brad says. 'Staff problems. Quite unavoidable. Please, sit down and have a coffee.'

'No, thank you,' Arthur says coldly. 'I only came to tell

you I won't be showing my paintings next month after all.'

'What?' Brad gasps.

'I won't be showing my paintings at the Courtney Art Gallery next month. Or any other month. There you are, I've told you. Good day.' Arthur turns away.

'But, Arthur,' Brad calls after him. 'Arthur!' But Arthur Grant has already gone.

Now it's Brad's turn to cover his face with his hands. 'I don't believe this,' he groans. 'How bad can a day get?'

There's silence for a while, and then, stupidly, I decide to speak. 'I wonder why he's decided to cancel the exhibition.'

Brad looks at me, and immediately I wish I had remained silent. 'Exactly what time did you arrive at work today, Alex?' he asks.

I look down at the table. 'Oh, er . . . more or less . . .'

'Just before I arrived myself?' Brad helps me out, and I nod my head, miserably.

There's silence for a while, then finally Brad speaks. 'Come back June Weatherby,' he says cruelly. '*Please*.' He finishes his coffee and walks to the door. 'Take the rest of the day off,' he says. 'And, Alex, make sure you get an early night tonight, won't you?' Then he turns and walks from the café, leaving me to pay the bill.

Chapter 2 *A bit about my peculiar family*

I *hate* June Weatherby. She reminds me of a girl who used to be in my class at school: Helen Peters. We children used to call her Saint Helen because she was so perfect at everything. The teachers all loved her, and somehow I know June Weatherby's school teachers loved her too.

I also know that neither June Weatherby nor Saint Helen would *ever* leave the house wearing different coloured shoes.

By now it's eleven o'clock. I pay for the coffee and leave the café. Brad's nowhere to be seen, and for a moment I wait on the pavement, wondering what to do with my unexpected day off work.

I don't actually *want* a day off, you see. Yes, I know that sounds crazy. Most people would be celebrating. But all it means to me is a whole day of not being with Brad. Even Brad laughing at my mistakes is better than no Brad at all.

A cold December wind's blowing straight off the sea. It's not a day to be standing around, so finally I start to walk towards home along the seafront. All the big old hotels are in this part of the town. They were built almost a hundred and fifty years ago, when Brighton first became a popular place for holidays, and they still look good today, especially with all their Christmas decorations up. I suppose the Grand Hotel's a bit ridiculous, but I do like it. Actually, I've always thought it looks a bit like a big white cake. A big white *wedding* cake.

Oh, how I wish I was the sort of girl who wakes up on time every morning. The sort of girl who always has a tidy flat and cupboards full of clean clothes. Someone who can cook delicious meals and organise perfect parties. *That* type of girl would be really useful at the Courtney Art Gallery, so useful in fact that Brad Courtney wouldn't be able to imagine life without her.

'Alex, hi!'

I'm so full of miserable thoughts that I don't see my friend Diana until I've almost walked into her. She's standing outside the Grand Hotel holding a huge bunch of flowers. That's her job, you see, delivering flowers. Her delivery van's parked on the road. It has a picture on the side of a man and a woman kissing. 'Kiss Flowers,' it says. 'For that perfect someone in your life.'

'Happy birthday!'

I try to smile. 'Thanks, Diana. Are those flowers for me?'

'Only if your name's Kitten.' She smiles.

'Kitten?' I ask.

'That's what it says on the card. To Kitten from Puppy,' Diana tells me.

I can tell what Diana thinks. She hates Kiss Flowers and is embarrassed to drive the van around. She's only doing the flower delivery job to save some money so she can travel to Africa to study rare animals.

'I think it's lovely,' I say, and she frowns at me.

'Don't tell me,' she says. 'You're thinking about that Brad Courtney, aren't you? You're wishing he would send you some Kiss Flowers. I bet you'd like him to call you Kitten.'

'If you met him, you'd understand,' I tell her. 'He's so –'

'So perfect, so fantastic. Yes, I know, you've told me several times before. Anyway, why aren't you at work?'

I frown, remembering the mystery of the locked gallery. 'I don't know,' I say. 'Brad gave me the day off. The gallery's closed.'

Diana doesn't think this is anything to worry about. 'Wonderful!' she says. 'You can do something really special on your birthday!'

'What?' I ask miserably, feeling sorry for myself. 'Everyone else is at work.'

'Go shopping,' Diana suggests.

'No money.'

'Well, go swimming then.' She tries again.

'No energy.'

'No money and no energy, OK.' Diana thinks for a while. 'I know, I could give you a lift to Rottingdean. That's where my next flower delivery is. You could visit your mother.'

I think about it for a while, wondering if this is really how I want to spend my birthday, and then I sigh. 'All right then, thanks.'

'OK. Just let me deliver these flowers to Kitten and I'll be right with you. Here, you can wait in the van.' Diana hands me the van keys and disappears inside the hotel.

At this point I think I'd better tell you something about my parents. You see, I love them both very much, but they're not exactly *relaxing* people. In fact, they're both a bit crazy – crazy and unusual. They don't live their lives the way other people live their lives. They don't even think the way other people think.

Actually, it's probably a good idea for you to meet them,

because then you'll understand why I sometimes find life so difficult myself.

One of my first memories ever is of a school sports day when I was about six years old. There was a school sports day every summer. We children ran in races, and our parents came to watch. All the mothers wore nice summer dresses with flower patterns on them and summer shoes.

My mother wore a flower-patterned dress too, but unfortunately she also wore flowers in her hair. *Lots* of them. And she didn't wear any shoes. None at all. Actually, when I was six years old I thought she looked very pretty, but I do still remember the other mothers looking at her and laughing. That's when I first realised she was different to other mothers.

Oh, by the way, Mum's name is Willow. (A willow is a type of tree that often grows close to rivers.) Dad's name is Moon. Moon is . . . well, you know what the moon is. These are my parents' 'earth' names. Their real names are Betty (Mum) and Jeff (Dad). They chose their earth names two years ago because they said they 'wanted to feel closer to nature'.

I've made it very clear to Mum and Dad that I *don't* want to have an earth name myself, but I still see Mum looking at me sometimes and I *know* she's thinking about names. When I'm not there, they probably call me Star or . . . Wood! But I'm quite happy with Alex, thank you! I don't even like Alexandra, which is my full name. My brother, Rob, lets Mum and Dad call him Tree, but then he lives hundreds of kilometres away in Scotland, so he doesn't see them very often. Besides, there aren't any trees on the Isle of Skye where he lives, so perhaps he feels his earth name is useful.

Diana is coming back out of the hotel now. To my surprise, she's still holding Kitten's flowers. 'Happy Birthday,' she says, getting into the van and giving the flowers to me.

'Didn't Kitten want them?' I ask, and she laughs.

'No, she didn't,' she says, starting the van. 'In fact, she told me she thought Puppy was a *dog*. She says she's given up men completely.'

'Poor Puppy!' I say, burying my nose in the flowers to smell them, but Diana doesn't seem to care.

'He probably only gave her flowers because he felt guilty about something,' she says.

I look at her as she turns the van round and we drive along the seafront towards the Palace Pier. 'Have you always hated men, Di?' I ask, and she seems quite surprised.

'Who says I hate men? I don't hate them. I just . . . well, pity them, I suppose. They're so weak compared to us women.'

I laugh. 'You just haven't met the right men, Di, that's all,' I tell her. 'Brad isn't weak at all.'

Diana smiles at me. 'Of course not. I was forgetting all about the wonderful, perfect, *strong* Mr Courtney!'

'Ha ha!' I know she's joking, but I don't mind. I like Diana. She's good for me because she's so confident. I've never known her to have any doubts about anything. She decided three years ago she wanted to study rare animals, and she's been working hard to save the money ever since. I'll really miss her when she leaves next year.

'Come on,' she says now. 'Tell me exactly what makes Brad Courtney so perfect. And don't just go on about his looks. You know they don't count for me. Some of the most interesting animals are the most ugly.'

'Well . . . Brad is rare, like one of your rare animals. There aren't many men like him around.'

'Come on, Alex. Try to tell me exactly what makes him so rare.'

I sigh. 'It's so difficult to put into words, Di. And there's no use saying that looks don't come into it, because they do. I don't know; when Brad enters a room it's suddenly different. I'd know he was there even if I was looking the other way. It's *chemical*.'

Diana still looks doubtful. 'You're talking about *lust*, not love, Alex. You just want to take him to bed and make love to him.'

I don't deny this, because it's true. I *do* want Brad to make love to me. But it isn't all I want.

'But those feelings of lust just don't last for long, do they?' she continues. 'Which is fine if you can accept that if you got involved with Brad it would just last for a few weeks. But I know you, you've probably got your wedding planned already.'

You see how well my friends know me?

'You've probably even thought of names for the children you're going to have with him.'

'People do meet, fall in love and get married!' I object, and she nods.

'Of course they do. And maybe I'm wrong about Brad, but I don't think so.'

'You haven't seen the way he looks at me sometimes, Di,'

19

I try to explain. 'It's as if . . . as if he sees right inside me and knows everything about me.' My face feels suddenly hot. 'It's as if he can . . . *see through my clothes.*'

Diana sighs again. 'OK,' she says, 'I give up. I tried to make you see sense, but I can see I'm wasting my time. Let's talk about something else. Your book. Have you started writing your book yet?'

I pull a face. You'll remember item number two on List Number One: the bestselling book. Diana's always asking me if I've started to write it. You see, if writing a bestselling book was something Diana wanted to do she would just sit down and do it. She wouldn't just *think about it* for years as I've done.

'No, not yet,' I reply.

'You should do,' she says. 'I bet you'd feel really good if you actually started to write it.'

The van has now left the houses of Brighton behind. Out of view far below us is the marina with its shops and boats, and next to us are green fields. In the holiday season people play games here, but today the grass is empty. Rottingdean is six kilometres from Brighton, and in the summer this road is busy with tourists and open-top buses. It's fun to sit at the top of the bus with the wind blowing through your hair from the sea. But I won't be catching an open-top bus home today. It's far too cold.

I sit quietly and think about what Diana said about my book. She might be wrong about Brad, but she is right about this. I would feel good if I started to write it. Yes. I'll make a start as soon as I get home from visiting Mum and Dad.

Perhaps I'll write an adventure story. Something really

exciting that could be turned into a film. About hidden gold in the jungle. There could be robbers and maybe a girl getting kidnapped. I could base the girl on me, only make her more beautiful and much braver. And the hero, the man who would fight the robbers and save the girl, well, the hero could be just like Brad . . .

Brad. It's useless. I can't think about anything but him. I sigh. Diana looks at me.

'Brad?' she asks, and I nod.

Diana shakes her head. 'Oh dear. Well, perhaps you should ask your mother for advice about Mr Courtney if you won't listen to me,' she suggests.

I look at her. 'Diana,' I say, 'you have met my mother, haven't you?'

She laughs. 'Oh yes,' she says. 'I was forgetting.'

Soon after this we arrive in Rottingdean and Diana stops outside my parents' house.

'By the way, Alex,' she says as I get out of the van, 'you do know you're wearing different coloured shoes, don't you?'

'It's the latest fashion,' I say. 'Didn't you know?'

Chapter 3 *Life should be like a colourful vase*

'Your Mr Courtney sounds fantastic,' my mother says and I smile, thinking how annoyed Diana would be if she could hear. 'Much better than Boring Barry.'

'Mum!'

'Well, sorry, darling. Barry's very nice of course, but he is a bit boring, you have to agree. I've always wanted you to have an *exciting* life. *He's* the type to want you to live in a small house in a small town and to have two children. A girl and a boy.'

'You had a girl and a boy!' I remind her. Today my mother's dressed in a short orange skirt and a red pullover. Her hair's orange too, and she's had it cut really short, like a boy's. For some reason she's wearing a red hat, even though she's indoors and the house is warm. She certainly isn't typical of people who live in Rottingdean. Neither is Dad. Mum noticed my odd shoes straight away, but she thought they looked really good. From now on she'll probably wear odd shoes herself.

'Yes, darling, I *did* have a boy and a girl. But I didn't mind if I had two girls or two boys or even three girls and three boys. The point is we didn't plan it all out the way Barry plans things out. We left it up to nature.'

Nature! How often have I heard *that* word from my mother I wonder?

Mum notices my expression. 'Don't look like that, darling. Nature's a wonderful thing! And your feelings for this Brad sound very natural to me. I'd *love* to meet him.'

No, no, no!

Poor Barry has met Mum and Dad a few times. Actually, he quite likes them, even though he thinks they're strange. They're always very nice to him. The poor man has no idea they think he's boring. But Brad! No, I can't imagine Brad meeting my parents at all. He thinks *I'm* strange enough.

'I haven't given you your birthday present yet,' Mum remembers, jumping up. As she goes out of the room I try to guess what the present will be. I've received some very unusual presents from Mum and Dad over the years, as I expect you can imagine: playing cards for telling my fortune; huge hairy hand-made pullovers; and once, when I was a child, a pet sheep. Actually, I loved the sheep. I called him Woolly Willy, and he lived in the back garden and kept the grass short.

'Here you are, darling,' Mum says, returning with the biggest vase I've ever seen. 'I made this for you myself.'

'Wow!' I hold out my arms for the vase. It's *really* heavy. 'Thank you, Mum.' The vase is blue. Well, a lot of it's blue, but it's also red and green. With yellow spots.

'I do hope you like it,' Mum's saying. 'I enjoyed making it.' She looks at me. 'In fact, darling, that vase is a lot like the life I'd like you to lead: exciting and colourful.'

I put the vase down on the floor and give my mother a kiss. 'I'll do my best, Mum,' I tell her. 'I'll do my best.'

When I set off for home later on, I get strange looks from passengers on a bus for the second time that day. This time I'm wearing odd shoes *and* I can hardly be seen from behind Mum's vase and Kitten's flowers. I almost expect the bus driver to ask me to buy a ticket for the vase since it is so large it needs its own seat.

Anyway, now you've met my mother, you can imagine, I'm sure, what it was like to grow up with such parents. Rob, my brother, is very like Mum and Dad. He never minded being different from other boys, and he's grown up to be a man who doesn't mind being different to other men. But as a child I always wished and wished to have a mother and father who were like everyone else's mother and father. I was terrified of becoming strange like them. I still am. Perhaps that's why I decided to be Barry's girlfriend in the first place; because he's ordinary.

And now I've fallen in love with someone who's far from ordinary. Perhaps I'm more like Mum than I like to think I am. In a few years' time I'll probably have orange hair and be proud of my earth name. And I'll probably still be wearing odd shoes.

When I finally get home after carrying the huge vase up the hill from the bus stop, it's three o'clock in the afternoon and I'm exhausted. Also, my head still hurts from last night's wine.

Maybe I should go to sleep for half an hour. Yes, that's the best thing to do. Then perhaps when I wake up I'll be more in the mood to go out and celebrate my birthday.

But when I wake up the room's in total darkness. I quickly switch on the light and look at the clock. Seven o'clock! I let out a small cry, 'Oh no!' I'm supposed to be meeting Barry in a restaurant at half past seven.

As I rush around getting changed I feel as if the morning's repeating itself. Only this time, before I leave the house, I make quite sure I'm wearing matching shoes.

I manage to stop a taxi and, much to my surprise, I arrive at the restaurant almost on time. Barry isn't there yet, which is odd because usually he's at least ten minutes early. As I'm almost always at least ten minutes late, he often has to wait twenty minutes for me. Strangely this never seems to make him cross.

Sometimes I'd *like* him to be cross. I know it seems silly, but Barry's far too nice to me. He isn't as boring as Mum says he is, but he is too nice. I'd probably like him a lot better if he shouted now and then the way Brad does.

Brad. There he is again, popping into my mind. Brad, Brad, Brad. I *can't* go on being Barry's girlfriend when all I do is think about Brad. It's cruel and selfish. I must tell Barry tonight that it's over. The only thing is, as it's my birthday, he'll probably arrive with a present for me. Oh, help.

Miserably I order a drink and sit at a table to wait, practising what to say to Barry in my mind.

'You see, Barry, I like you very much, but . . .'

'Barry, I'm sorry, but I've met someone else.'

'Barry, thanks so much for the lovely present, but actually, I've decided . . .'

Oh no, this is going to be *awful*.

Just then a woman comes in. As she walks past my table I smell her perfume. It's very familiar. She sits facing me at a table in the far corner of the restaurant and I recognise her straight away. Tania Stevenson. *Brad's girlfriend.*

This is definitely the worst birthday I've ever had.

Quickly I pick up a menu and hide behind it, looking at Tania over the top. She's wearing a dress I saw in a shop a few weeks ago, a dress that was far too expensive for me to

25

buy. It cost more than I earn at the gallery in a week. Her blonde shoulder-length hair is perfect (of course) and so is her make-up.

Suddenly, I feel very untidy. I've brushed my hair, but it would never look as perfect as Tania's, even if I brushed it for a whole hour. The little black dress I'm wearing is over a year old and a bit too tight for me at the moment. My weight's always changing, you see. Sometimes I'm quite thin, but more often I'm a little fat. I take after my mother that way. The difference is, my mother doesn't mind, whereas I do.

I need a cigarette. I definitely need a cigarette. OK, I know I've given up, but this is a *crisis*. Did I bring any cigarettes with me? Yes, surely I did! I begin to search anxiously in my handbag, but just then I notice the 'no smoking' signs everywhere around the restaurant. OK, I can manage without a cigarette. Yes, of course I can! I *can*! I'll just have to drink more wine, that's all.

I continue to watch Tania over the top of my menu and see her take a lipstick from her bag. Very carefully she paints her lips bright red, and I wonder if Brad will be kissing those lips later on.

Brad! If Tania's here, then Brad will probably be arriving any minute! And suddenly I remember him asking me to telephone to reserve a table for him at this restaurant. How could I have forgotten? I *hated* doing it.

'I thought I told you to get an early night, Alex,' says a familiar voice at my shoulder, and there he is, looking more handsome than ever in a smart grey suit.

'I know,' I say, my mouth suddenly dry with nervousness. 'But I couldn't.'

He's looking at me in that way I told Di about earlier on, his dark eyes staring straight into mine as if I'm the only person in the restaurant.

'You couldn't?' he repeats. 'I see. Someone came round to your house and forced you to come out, perhaps. They had a gun, did they? Or was it a knife?'

He's joking, of course. The trouble is, when he makes jokes like this I can *never* think of anything clever or funny to say back to him. Anyway, Tania's calling to him from across the restaurant.

'Brad! I'm over here, Brad!'

He looks up and waves at her. 'Well,' he says to me, 'if you're still sitting here at ten o'clock, I'm going to get a gun out myself and force you to go home, OK?' He walks away before I can answer and the next moment he's ruining Tania's lipstick with a kiss. I don't want to look, but somehow I can't help it.

'Who is that, darling?' Tania asks in a loud voice, and when Brad looks my way, my face goes red.

'She's my temporary assistant,' he tells Tania, emphasising the word temporary. 'You met her a few weeks ago.'

'Oh,' Tania says, sounding bored. 'I don't remember. What a horrible dress she's wearing. You ought to pay her more money, Brad.'

I sit there unhappily, listening to Tania laugh. It's all very confusing. I don't understand how Brad can look at me the way he does and then let Tania be so horrible about me. And suddenly I wish Barry would get here. Boring but nice Barry who thinks I look good whatever I'm wearing.

But suddenly I realise Barry's never going to come

here. Because this isn't the restaurant we arranged to meet in . . .

'Oh, no!' I push back my chair and get up so quickly I manage to drop my handbag. My purse falls out and coins roll everywhere: under tables, under handbags, under feet.

'Oh, *no!*' I start to pick the money up, apologising to people as I reach under their tables.

'Collecting change for the bus, Alex?' says a familiar voice, causing me to bang my head on a table.

'Careful,' Brad advises, holding out a twenty-pence piece that has rolled right across the room. Standing up and rubbing my head, I look at him, knowing Tania is still laughing at me.

I take the coin from his fingers. 'Er . . . thank you.' I'm just trying to think of something, *anything*, more interesting to say, something to make him realise that *I'm* the woman of his dreams, not Tania, when the restaurant door opens and a bunch of Kiss Flowers walks in.

'Alex!' says Barry's voice from behind the flowers. 'I've been searching for you in every restaurant in town! Happy birthday!'

Chapter 4   *Talking isn't always easy*

It's still my thirtieth birthday – yes, doesn't time pass slowly when you're having fun? Barry has suggested we stay in this restaurant now, so here we are, sitting at a table for two with romantic music playing in the background. Brad and Tania the Terrible are still here. I can see them looking into each other's eyes at their own table for two at the other end of the room.

This is how I'm feeling: Old. Fat. Foolish. Jealous.

You'll probably be thinking that things can't get any worse. If you are, then you're quite wrong. Barry's looking at me with a pleased kind of expression on his face.

'What is it?' I ask, feeling immediately suspicious, but just as I do I notice that the entire restaurant staff are walking towards me, smiling in just the same way Barry's smiling. They stop a metre or so away from our table, all except one girl who's holding a large bunch of balloons.

'Happy birthday, Alex,' she says, and ties the balloons to the back of my chair. Then she steps back to join the rest of the staff and they all start to sing. Very loudly.

'Happy birthday to you. Happy birthday to you. Happy birthday, dear Alex. Happy birthday to you!'

The balloons surround my face: green, blue, yellow and red. I want to die.

Then, just when I think the nightmare's over, one of the waiters gives a cough before making an announcement.

'Ladies and gentlemen,' he shouts, so loudly Mum and

Dad can probably hear him in Rottingdean. 'Today is Alex Faye's thirtieth birthday! Thirty today! Three cheers for Alex!'

Then everybody in the restaurant joins in. 'Hooray!' they cheer. 'Hooray! Hooray!'

I try to speak. I'm only able to whisper very very quietly. 'Thank you,' I say. 'Thank you very much.'

Over on the other side of the restaurant I can see Brad and Tania laughing, and now I can add something else to my list of how I'm feeling: embarrassed.

I now feel old, fat, foolish, jealous and embarrassed.

Thank you Barry. Thank you life. Thank you very much.

On the other side of the table, I notice that Barry's still looking pleased with himself. He has no idea how I feel at all. He thinks – he *actually* thinks – he's done something special for me. Barry has been my boyfriend for two years. *Two years*. And he has no idea at all that this is the worst day of my entire life.

'Good news!' he says, spreading butter on some bread. 'My company heard today from the Council about that work for the motorway bridges. We got it!'

'Good,' I say automatically, watching him eat his bread. I don't feel at all hungry at the moment myself. In fact, right now I don't feel as if I shall ever want to eat anything again. This is funny in a way, because Barry and I actually met because of a plate of food.

I was at a friend's wedding party, and there was lots of delicious food. I was very hungry so I had piled my plate with food and, I'm sure you've already guessed it, I dropped the plate. Some of the food landed on my new dress, but most of it went on Barry. The messiest food went on Barry.

Amazingly, he didn't shout at me. You see, even then he was too nice! We just found a kitchen and cleaned our clothes up a little and then we sat and chatted. Barry was really interested in everything I had to say. I liked that.

'It does mean I'll be working away from home for a while though,' he's saying to me now. 'We won't see so much of each other for a few weeks.'

This is my chance to tell him. I lick my lips, feeling suddenly nervous. Then when I'm just about to speak, I suddenly notice something happening at Brad and Tania's table, something that makes me feel very happy indeed. Brad and Tania are having an argument!

'Alex?' Barry says. 'Didn't you hear what I said? I said I'll miss you.'

'Yes, yes,' I say impatiently, trying to hear Brad and Tania's conversation.

'It's not my fault, Tania,' I can hear him saying. 'I had no idea. No idea at all. Believe me.'

'But what will people *think*?' Tania cries. 'Everyone will be talking about it! It's horrible. *Horrible*!'

What? What will everyone be talking about? What's horrible? *What*?

'Alex?'

'Hmm?' I realise Barry's speaking to me.

'I asked you if you would miss me too.'

'Yes, yes, of course I will,' I answer without thinking, looking at the couple on the far side of the room. As I watch, Tania gets to her feet. Picking up her handbag, she walks quickly away from the table. Brad gets up more slowly, putting some money down on the table before he starts to follow her.

'Good,' I'm only faintly conscious of Barry saying to me as Tania walks past us, 'because I really care about you, Alex, I really do.'

'What?' I'm not listening to Barry because Brad's walking towards me now, and he's looking at me. Even in the middle of a crisis he's staring at me in that special way. It must mean something. It *must*!

He stops briefly at our table. 'Happy birthday, Alex,' he says in his attractive deep voice. 'Remember, don't stay up too late!' Then he leaves the restaurant.

'Who was that?' Barry asks.

'My boss.'

'Oh.' Barry looks thoughtful for a while, then smiles. 'They don't seem very happy, do they?' he says. 'Not like us. We never argue, do we?'

*   *   *

I wake up the next morning feeling terrible. Not because I drank too much wine last night this time, but just because I don't like myself very much. Barry has gone away to build bridges for motorways with no idea that I don't want to be his girlfriend any longer. If I ever do write my adventure book it will be impossible to base the character of the girl on myself. I'm too frightened even to talk to my boyfriend.

Still, I've woken up early enough to walk to work for once, so after checking that my shoes are the same colour, I leave my flat and walk down the street to the seafront.

Even feeling as miserable as I do, I notice the sea looks almost as blue as it does in the summer. It's a beautiful day, cold but sunny with only a gentle wind. It isn't a day to feel miserable for long, and by the time I reach the Grand Hotel the sunshine has cheered me up.

I wonder if Kitten's still staying at the hotel and whether she has forgiven Puppy yet. And then I remember Brad and Tania's argument and smile. I still have no idea what it was about, but it really did sound serious. Perhaps they have broken up. Perhaps Brad's now a free man!

Feeling suddenly keen to arrive at work, I begin to walk faster. If Brad and Tania have broken up, he'll probably be a little sad for a while I suppose. He'll need someone to talk to. As I hurry along, I imagine him talking to me about it. Perhaps we'll go to the Sea View Café again, or maybe we'll just sit in the gallery. Anyway, it will just be me and him. I'll listen to him. I'll be understanding. (Though not *too* understanding.) He'll look into my eyes as he talks, and suddenly he'll realise he doesn't care about breaking up with Tania after all . . .

By the time I reach Ship Street I'm so anxious to arrive at work, I'm practically running. I rush around the corner and . . . bang straight into someone.

'Brad!'

'For goodness' sake, Alex!' Brad is standing in the middle of the pavement, and he has to reach out to stop me from falling over. 'Can't you look where you're going?'

'Sorry,' I say breathlessly. 'I didn't see you.'

'Obviously not.' He lets go of my arms but doesn't start walking. Instead he turns to look up the road in the direction of the gallery, and I suddenly get the feeling that something's wrong.

'What is it?' I ask, and when he points, I notice a small

33

crowd of people standing outside the gallery. They all seem to be holding cameras.

'Who are they?' I ask, feeling puzzled, and Brad frowns.

'Journalists,' he says. 'Come on, we'll get into the gallery round the back.' And the next moment he has turned down a narrow path between two buildings.

'Brad,' I say, following him, 'what's going on?'

'Shh!' He hurries along, keeping close to the wall as if he's a private detective in a film. Either that or a criminal on the run from the police!

'Brad, are you in some sort of trouble?' I ask, but he doesn't answer and just keeps on hurrying along the narrow pathway. I can smell food – fish – and realise we're now behind the fish restaurant. The path is taking us behind the shops and restaurants in Ship Street. Yes, there's the back of the art gallery.

'I wish you'd tell me what's happening,' I say.

'Shh!' he says as he looks around, and I realise he's checking to see if there are any journalists about.

By now I'm almost dying of curiosity. Yesterday was strange enough with the gallery being closed, but this is a real mystery. And suddenly I remember Tania's words in the restaurant last night. 'What will people *think*?' she said. And, 'Everyone will be talking about it!' There must be some connection between these journalists and what she was talking about.

But what?

Chapter 5 *The wrong pictures*

'I'll open the door,' Brad whispers. 'You go in first. I'll lock the door behind us. But stay in the back office. Don't let them see you.'

Feeling more and more as if I'm acting in a film, I do as he says, and soon we're both in the small office at the back of the art gallery with the door locked.

'I'll close the curtains,' he says, still whispering, and soon the room's in darkness.

I realise that the only sound I can hear is Brad's breathing. We're quite alone together, just me and Brad in the darkness. And I know exactly what advice my mother would give me if she were here. 'Move as close to him as you can,' she would say, 'and *he might kiss you.*'

So I do move a bit closer, but Brad doesn't seem to notice.

'I expect you want to know what all this is about,' he says.

'Er . . . what?' It's difficult to concentrate. My head's so filled with pictures of him kissing me.

In the darkness I hear Brad sigh. 'I said I expect you want to know what all this is about.'

'Oh, er . . . yes. Yes, please.'

'Read this,' he says, handing me a newspaper.

There's just enough light coming through the curtains for me to read the headline:

'BRIGHTON GALLERY IN FORGERY SCANDAL.'

'What?' I can't believe my eyes. *Forgery scandal?* 'What does it mean?' I ask again.

Brad's face looks worried. 'Those Ralph Blackman paintings I bought,' he says, 'they turned out to be fakes.'

'Fakes?' I repeat the word stupidly, and he frowns at me.

'Yes, fakes,' he says very slowly as if I'm a child. 'You know, painted by someone who isn't Ralph Blackman but signed with Ralph Blackman's name.'

'I know what a fake is,' I say a little crossly.

'Good,' he says. 'Then you also know what trouble is. And police questioning. Something like this is terrible for business. We'll lose our good name. Arthur Grant won't be the only artist to leave the gallery.'

'You've been questioned by the police?'

'Yes, most of yesterday. I told them I didn't know about the paintings. I'm not sure they believe me, though.'

'They won't send you to prison, will they?' I say worriedly. Brad's face looks worse than ever, and I realise he hasn't thought about the possibility of going to prison. Why can't I *think* before I speak?

'I don't know,' he says, sounding really unhappy.

'But you didn't know the paintings were fakes! You really thought Ralph Blackman had painted them. If anyone goes to prison it should be the person who sold them to you!' I say, hoping to make him feel better.

Brad bought the paintings during my first week at the gallery. I remember it well because I thought they were horrible dark pictures of trees and fields in the rain. I didn't say anything about not liking them at the time though. Well, Brad said Ralph Blackman was a famous artist you

see, and I didn't want him to know I had never heard of
him.

Brad was very pleased because he had bought the
paintings so cheaply. The very next week he sold them
again for double the money to an American. But now it
turns out that they were fakes, not real Ralph Blackmans at
all.

'Is this what Tania was so worried about?' I ask him, but
when he looks at me I wish I hadn't. He looks sort of . . .
dangerous.

'What do you mean?' he asks. 'How do you know about
that?'

My face is going red again. I can feel it.

'Well, last night, I . . . I wasn't listening. I just . . .
heard. She . . . Tania wasn't exactly speaking quietly, was
she?'

He looks at me for a while, then sighs. 'No, I suppose
you're right, she wasn't. And yes, this is what she was so
worried about. Tania's father's a judge. She was worried
about what he would say if this was in the newspapers.' As
he speaks he pushes one hand through his hair. It's
something he often does when he's thinking. I love the way
it makes his hair all untidy.

I look away from him, trying to concentrate. I know it's
important to say the right thing now, and I can't afford to
be thinking about Brad's hair. 'Well,' I say, taking a deep
breath, 'if you want to know what I think then . . . well, I
think Tania should *know* this isn't your fault. She should
know you wouldn't do something like this on purpose. You
aren't a criminal!'

There is silence in the room for a while after my little

speech. I wonder if I've said too much. After all, Tania is his girlfriend. Or at least, she was.

Just then we both hear a noise from next door. One of the journalists is shouting through the letterbox.

'Mr Courtney, can you tell us how many of the paintings in your gallery at the moment are fakes?'

'How dare they?' Brad says angrily, and the next moment he's opening the door to the art gallery and rushing through.

'None of the pictures in this art gallery are fakes!' I hear him shout, and I quickly follow him into the gallery. Outside I can see the journalists going crazy. There are perhaps ten or twelve, and they're staring at us through the glass windows as if we're animals in a zoo. Some are taking photographs and some are banging on the glass, shouting.

'Mr Courtney, look this way, please!'

'Is it true the police arrested you yesterday, Mr Courtney?'

'What does Judge Stevenson think about this, Mr Courtney?'

I move to stand next to Brad and instantly the cameras are pointed in my direction too. 'Perhaps we should just leave, Brad,' I suggest, but he won't hear of it.

'No,' he says angrily, 'not until I've killed these fools!'

'Murder wouldn't be very good publicity for the gallery,' I say, taking his arm to lead him back to the office. 'Come on, let's just go.'

But when we get into the office we find the journalists have discovered the back entrance to the gallery.

'Mr Courtney!' they shout, banging on the back door. We're trapped.

'Now what do we do?' I ask, and Brad runs both hands through his hair, thinking.

'I know what I'd *like* to do,' he replies, 'but I suppose we're just going to have to walk through them. Unless we want to spend the next forty-eight hours trapped in this office, that is.'

'Yes, please!' I think, but Brad is already planning our escape.

'OK, here's what we'll do,' he says. 'We'll walk straight out of the front door and we'll say nothing to them except "no comment". Whatever they say to us, that's all we say, OK? "No comment".'

'No comment,' I say, practising, and he nods.

'Good.' Then he leads the way back into the gallery.

As he unlocks the door the journalists are all shouting questions at him, and when we go outside they crowd around us, shouting and taking photographs.

'Mr Courtney! Mr Courtney!'

'Miss! Can I ask who you are, Miss?'

I look at the journalist who asked the question. 'No comment,' I say. 'No comment!'

We start to walk down Ship Street, but they follow us, so Brad takes my hand. 'Come on,' he says, 'let's run.'

We start to run. So do the journalists. I wish my mother could see me. She would definitely like the way my life has suddenly become so exciting! I'm really enjoying myself!

'Quickly, get into my car,' says Brad when we reach the seafront. I jump in beside him and he starts the engine. As we drive quickly off, I look over my shoulder. The journalists are standing in a disappointed group on the corner of Ship Street.

Chapter 6   *Hill View House*

'We lost them!' I cheer, but Brad's still frowning.

'For now,' he says. 'For now.'

But I refuse to be calm. 'This is so exciting!' I say, and this time his frown is rather cool.

'I'm very glad my personal disaster is so entertaining, Alex,' he says.

Oh dear. 'I didn't mean that, Brad,' I tell him quickly. 'I don't *want* you to be in trouble, it's just that . . . well, this is so much more interesting than sitting in the gallery answering the telephone and watching people walk by outside.'

'Your job is to help me to sell paintings, Alex,' he reminds me, 'not to watch tourists.'

Oh. Me and my big mouth!

Brad gives a little laugh, and I decide it's probably best to keep quiet for a while. I'm so busy thinking about everything that's just happened that it isn't until some time later that I realise I don't know where we're going.

'Brad?'

'What?'

'Where are we going?' I ask.

He stops at some traffic lights and looks at me. 'To get some country air. I need to think.'

'Oh,' I say, feeling suddenly happy. 'Lovely.'

A day out in the countryside with Brad! There's no

need at all for him to take me with him, but he obviously wants to. He wants to be with me. *He wants to be with me!* I'm so happy I feel like singing. Then I remember my shoes. As I told you, they're the same colour today, but unfortunately they aren't flat sensible shoes, suitable for walking in the countryside. They're fashion shoes. And I've already done that long walk from my flat to Ship Street in them. In short, my feet hurt.

'What's wrong?' Brad asks.

'Nothing,' I say, but too late. Brad has already seen me looking doubtfully down at my feet.

He smiles. 'Oh, Alex, Alex, Alex,' he says. 'Do you ever wear the right shoes?' Then he starts to laugh, but you know, somehow I don't mind this time. This laughter's somehow different. Friendly. *Warm.*

So I laugh too. 'Not often,' I say.

I always love driving away from Brighton into the countryside. Don't misunderstand me. I love living in Brighton. It's a lively town with lots to do and see. It's just that sometimes, in the summer, it feels a little as if the tourists have stolen the town from those of us who live there all year round. They walk slowly along by the sea with their ice creams, wearing silly hats, and then they all travel home again at the same time in the evening, blocking the roads and filling the trains.

When the tourists stop coming in the autumn, it feels as if we get the town back again. This is when it's fun to cycle along the seafront (past the 'no cycling' signs), or to walk to Rottingdean past the marina and along the path next to the sea. When the sea's rough, the waves hit the wall by the side of the path and shoot right up into the air. If you don't run fast enough, you get very wet. Running from the waves is a game I really enjoy.

When Brad's my boyfriend, I'll suggest we play the running from the waves game. It's like being a child again, but it can also be quite romantic because you can scream and hold onto each other. Once, when I played the game with Barry, we both got *really* wet.

But I don't want to think about Barry or I'll start to feel guilty again.

'Was that your boyfriend you were with last night?' Brad asks just then, and I look at him, wondering if he can read my thoughts. I hope not!

'Er . . . that was Barry, he's just a friend,' I lie. Although it isn't a complete lie. You see, I do like Barry. I'd be very sad if I thought I'd never see him again. I'd really like us to stay friends.

'And it was your thirtieth birthday.'

'How did you guess that?' I joke, remembering the balloons and the singing.

'Alex,' Brad says, 'thirty isn't old. You're just a baby.' And he leans forward to switch on some music.

'Thanks!' I say, happily, wondering how old he is. I don't ask him though. I'm too afraid to! But I'd guess . . . maybe thirty-seven or thirty-eight. Definitely not older than that. Just the right age for me.

We drive past Lewes, a pretty little market town with a ruined castle, and then the road heads into the green hills. These hills are called the South Downs, and they always remind me of the backbone of some ancient large animal. They're beautiful at all times of the year.

The weather over the Downs can sometimes be different from the weather in Brighton, even though the town isn't very far away. It's like that today. In Brighton it was sunny, but here it's grey and the Downs look very dark against the sky. To tell you the truth, the scene looks a bit like a Ralph Blackman painting, and I think Brad thinks so too. Anyway, he's frowning again, and suddenly he reaches forward to switch off the cheerful music.

'It's damn well going to rain,' he says.

'Yes,' I have to agree, 'it does look like it.' I hope Brad will change his mind about going for a walk if it does rain. It's true that I don't mind getting wet by the sea. That's fun. But walking through mud in unsuitable shoes isn't fun. No fun at all.

Through the car window I can see Firle Beacon, the highest point along this part of the Downs. The cloud's so low by now it's hiding the hilltop completely. We pass a farm shop by the side of the road. There are Christmas trees for sale outside. I look at them with a sense of surprise, wondering if it will ever feel like Christmas this year.

Suddenly Brad slows the car down, and my heart sinks. I try to tell myself it won't be so bad. That rain, mud and cold will be fun if I'm with Brad, but somehow I can't quite believe it.

The car turns right, travelling up a narrow rough road in the direction of Firle Beacon, and when we go round a corner, I can see a house ahead. The house is dark-looking, but then everything looks dark by now. It looks as if it's about to rain very heavily indeed.

The road stops at the house, and to my great surprise, so does the car.

'Where are we?' I ask, but Brad's already getting out.

'I should hurry up if you don't want to get wet,' he says, and then to my amazement he takes a key from his pocket and walks up to the house.

I follow him slowly. There's a sign outside. 'Hill View House'.

'Do you live here?' I ask, joining him in the hall.

'Sometimes,' he says. 'This place belonged to my grandmother. She was a friend of the Bloomsbury Group.' He looks at me. 'You have heard of the Bloomsbury Group, haven't you?'

'Yes, of course.' I really have, actually. Most people who live in this area have. The Bloomsbury Group was a group of artists who lived and worked together in the 1930s. They had a house called Charleston which is near here. Barry and I visited it once. I think he thought it was a bit crazy, but I thought it was beautiful. The whole house is decorated with paintings: the doors, the walls, even the furniture!

Brad looks at me doubtfully. 'Hmm,' he says. 'Well, anyway, my grandmother bought this house intending to turn it into another Charleston, but unfortunately she was no artist. She was happy here though. This is where my mother was born. I came here for holidays as a boy.'

I immediately have a picture of him as a little boy in my mind, wearing short trousers, his black hair untidy.

'It's a lovely house,' I say, and Brad nods.

'Yes, I think so. Not everyone wants to live in the countryside though.'

I can't imagine Tania living here at all. It's much too far away from fashion shops and smart café bars.

44

'I could live here,' I tell him without thinking, and he looks at me.

What he says next takes me totally by surprise. 'Well,' he says, 'that's interesting because I was going to ask you if you would. At least, not *live* here, but stay here. For tonight, anyway. I don't want to go back to Brighton today. Of course, if you don't want to stay, I could drive you to Lewes and you could catch a train back to Brighton.'

Wow, wow, wow! Me and Brad alone in this wonderful place. I can't believe my luck.

'No,' I say quickly. 'No, that would be fine. I mean, I'd like to stay.'

'I always want to paint when the rest of my life is in a mess,' he says, taking off his coat and hanging it up. 'This is where I have my studio.'

'You're an artist?' I ask, amazed.

'Yes, I'm an artist.' He holds out his hand for my coat. 'Why's that so surprising?'

'I don't know. I mean, it isn't!' I'm embarrassed again, but Brad's smiling.

'It's all right, Alex. You weren't to know.' He hangs up my coat and goes into the kitchen to put the kettle on. When I follow him, I see that the kitchen's painted a warm yellow with a red-brown floor. Very Mediterranean-looking. Nice.

'Come on,' Brad says, 'I'll show you my paintings while we wait for the water to boil.'

As I follow him up the stairs I feel really excited. I'm finding so much out about Brad today. So much has happened, and it's still only eleven o'clock.

'This is the studio,' he says, leading the way into a big

45

square room with very large windows.

'Oh, what a fantastic view!' I say, crossing to the window to look out. Outside the skies are still dark, but it hasn't started to rain yet. But even in this poor light the view of Firle Beacon is wonderful. The room is perfect for an artist.

Brad doesn't seem interested in the view. I can hear him moving things around in the room behind me, and when I turn round I notice several paintings leaning against the wall. They're all facing the wrong way, but because of the view from the window, I guess they will be landscapes. I'm so sure about it that when Brad turns two round the right way, I can't help but gasp with surprise.

'What is it?' he asks, frowning at me. 'Don't you like them?'

For a moment I can't think of anything to say. The paintings aren't landscapes at all. To be honest, I've no idea *what* they are. One of them seems to be completely black except for a small green spot in one corner, and the other seems to be all white. *All* white. It doesn't even have any spots.

'Yes!' I cry quickly. 'Of course I like them! They're . . .' But I have to stop because I can't think how to continue the sentence. Panicking a little, I start another one. 'Is . . . is that one a snow scene?' I ask.

My question is followed by a long silence. It's as quiet as it was in the gallery office. I can hear his breathing again.

Brad's frowning. I realise I've made a big mistake.

'No, Alex,' he says at last, 'it's not a snow scene. It's not a *scene* at all. I'm not a landscape painter.'

'Oh,' I say, swallowing nervously. 'Sorry. I . . . I don't know much about modern art.'

'So it would seem.' Brad returns his paintings to their place against the wall as if I'm no longer allowed to see them. 'And yet, if I remember correctly, when you came to the job interview, you told me you knew a lot about art.'

It's true. I did say that. OK, I lied. But you see, as soon as I saw Brad, I knew I had to get the job. I was a desperate girl, and I took desperate action.

'I . . . well, I do know about art,' I say. 'Well, a bit, anyway. Just . . . just not modern art.'

'OK, who's your favourite artist?' he demands to know.

By now I'm panicking so much that for a moment the only artist's name I can remember is Ralph Blackman's. Luckily I realise it wouldn't be a good idea to say his name though, and I think for a little while longer.

'Van Gogh!' I shout at last, and he looks at me doubtfully.

'OK,' he says. 'Name three paintings by Van Gogh.'

'Um . . .' I say, thinking hard.

'Two paintings.'

'Um . . .'

'Come on, Alex! *One* painting.'

Suddenly I remember one, and shout out its name excitedly. '*Sunflowers!*'

Brad doesn't seem to be impressed. He shakes his head. 'Alex, every person in the world has heard of *Sunflowers*,' he says.

'Well, I haven't got a very good memory for names,' I say weakly. 'That's why I can't think of any more titles.'

'Hmm,' he says, 'I'm not sure I entirely believe you, Alex, but never mind. Go and make the coffee while I get my paints ready, would you?'

By the time I return with the coffee Brad's staring hard at his white painting. In fact, he hardly notices I'm there. He just takes his coffee and keeps right on staring.

I stare at the painting too, trying to see more in it than just white. Eventually I notice that it's painted in three or four different types of white: blue-white, grey-white, green-white and . . . plain white. The more I look, the more I see. Some of the paint's thick, and some of the paint's thin. The different whites look a bit like rocks covered by snow.

Brad might not think he has painted a snow scene, but I still think he has. Not that I intend to say that to him though!

'Go for a walk or something won't you, Alex?' Brad says to me over his shoulder. 'I prefer to be alone when I'm painting.'

I look out of the window. It is now raining *very hard indeed*. Firle Beacon has almost disappeared from view.

'Or if you don't want to do that,' he continues, 'why don't you find yourself a book to read? There are plenty in the sitting-room. I'll be about two or three hours here.'

So I wander downstairs, trying not to feel fed up. If Tania were here instead of me, would it be different? Would he send *her* downstairs to read a book while he painted a picture? Somehow I can't imagine it.

Chapter 7 *Alone with Brad*

In the sitting-room the books on the shelves look boring. Besides, I don't feel like reading. I've got too much on my mind. Being alone overnight here with Brad is my big chance to make something happen between us. I can't waste it.

'Alex,' I tell myself, 'you need a *plan.*'

Then suddenly I have a brilliant idea. I'll cook a really special meal. A meal so delicious that when Brad tastes it, he'll see that *I* can be creative too.

I hurry to the kitchen to check the fridge. Chicken, carrots, mushrooms, potatoes . . . Excellent! I can make a chicken casserole.

Singing happily to myself, I set to work preparing the vegetables and chopping up the chicken. Casseroles are perfect for a cold wet winter's day. They warm you up. Also, they are very easy to make, as you'll know if you've ever made one. All you have to do is throw the ingredients into a dish, add a little water, put the dish into the oven and leave it to cook for a few hours. It's impossible for anything to go wrong.

In fact, the casserole is so easy to prepare that after twenty minutes I have nothing to do again. Outside it's still raining heavily, so I go back into the sitting-room to give Brad's books a second chance. I take down an art book but soon put it back on the shelf. It contains pictures of paintings that look a lot like Brad's. Actually, I really hate to admit it, but I'm very disappointed by Brad's paintings. I like Brad so much, I want to like his paintings too, and . . . well, I don't. I don't even think Mum would like them, actually. She likes a lot of modern art, but I think even she would say Brad's pictures were *boring*. But I don't want to think about it, because the words 'boring' and 'Brad' just don't go together in my mind.

I choose a detective story and take it over to the sofa. But I'm afraid that by the time I finish reading a few pages of the dull detective's dull inquiries, I'm asleep. So deeply asleep I don't wake up until I hear Brad calling my name, and by then the room's dark.

'Alex,' Brad calls down the stairs, 'I'm sure I can smell something burning.'

The casserole! I jump up and run wildly from the room.

'What's wrong?' Brad asks me from the landing, but I don't stop.

'Nothing, nothing!' I say, running down the hall.

Brad doesn't seem to believe me. He hurries downstairs and arrives in the smoke-filled kitchen shortly after I do. 'Bloody hell!' he swears. 'What have you been *doing*, Alex?'

As I open the oven door even more smoke fills the room. 'Just a bit of cooking,' I say. 'Cooking and . . . sleeping.'

I'm sure I don't need to tell you that the evening doesn't turn out the way I'd planned it at all. The only food left in the house is two frozen lasagnes, which Brad heats up in the microwave. I offer to do it, but he won't allow me to.

'No!' he says. 'You'd probably blow the microwave up!' And by now I feel such a failure, I almost think he's right.

I had intended to serve my wonderful meal in the dining room with soft lights and nice music. A romantic background for what – I hoped – would be a romantic evening.

Instead, we eat our heated-up lasagnes in the sitting-room, watching a quiz show on television.

I hate quiz shows. Well, that's not quite true. What I hate about quiz shows is not knowing the answers to *any* of the questions. If I knew as many answers as Brad obviously does, then perhaps I would like quiz shows as much as he seems to like them.

Here we are, alone in the countryside, sitting next to each other on the sofa. And yet the situation is definitely not romantic.

'Michael Faraday!' shouts Brad in answer to the question: 'Who first thought of the electric light bulb?'

And 'Champs-Elysées!' to the question: 'On what famous street does the *Tour de France* cycle race end?'

It's only too obvious he's completely forgotten that I'm sitting next to him at all.

'Perhaps you ought to write to the television company to ask if you can appear on the quiz show,' I suggest.

Brad watches as a woman on the television wins ten thousand pounds. 'I'll probably have to do just that with the trouble the gallery's in at the moment,' he sighs. 'I've got to pay the customer who bought those fake Ralph Blackman paintings a lot of money soon, and I'm not certain I can afford it.' He looks at me. 'Actually, Alex,' he says, 'I'm not sure I can afford *you* any longer, to be honest. As from tomorrow I'm going to have to manage without an assistant.'

What? I stare at him. 'You mean . . . you don't want me to work for you any more?'

'The job was only temporary,' he reminds me. 'I'm just ending it sooner than I thought I would. I know it's almost Christmas, but I'm afraid I have no choice.'

I sit there with my dirty lasagne plate on my knees, feeling totally shocked.

'It's a pity really,' Brad says. 'Of course, you were about as useful to me in the gallery as you seem to be in a kitchen, but you are pleasant to look at. June isn't. Oh, June's very well-organised but she *isn't* pretty.'

My mind is finding it difficult to manage. It's trying to deal with two very different shocks at the same time: one nasty shock and one *fantastic* shock. 'You . . . you really think I'm pretty?' I ask at last, preferring to think about the fantastic shock rather than the nasty shock.

'Well,' he says, looking at me, 'perhaps not *quite* so pretty as usual with your mouth open the way it is at the moment.' (I quickly close my mouth.) 'But usually, yes, I think you are pretty. Of course, you have your faults. I mean, your hair's often messy, and some of your clothes are –'

'Don't spoil it!' I say quickly, and he smiles.

'Anyway, I'm afraid the fact that you're pretty doesn't help me to pay that customer the money I owe him, so I'm sorry, but . . .'

'I have to go,' I finish his sentence for him.

'Yes.'

'Right.'

I'm not doing very well at achieving the things on my list, am I? I'm *not* married to Brad. I'm *not* engaged to Brad. I'm *not* even his girlfriend. And as from tomorrow I'm not even going to be employed by him.

'You aren't going to cry, are you?' he asks, sounding worried. 'I'm not very good with women who cry.'

And suddenly I feel as if I might be very close to tears. 'No,' I say, my voice shaking a little, 'I'm not . . . going to . . . cry.' But then I *am* crying. I can't help it.

Brad groans. 'Hell,' he says, and takes the dirty plate from my knees and puts it on the floor. 'Come here, you silly thing,' he says, and he looks deep into my red eyes.

'It really isn't anything to cry about,' he says softly, but it's no use, I can't stop crying. In fact, it seems worse with him being so nice to me.

'Oh, Alex, please. Don't cry,' he says, and then . . . *he puts his arm around me.*

I'm so surprised I stop crying almost immediately. Ever since I first met Brad I've wanted him to hold me in his arms, and now, at last, it's happened. It's not the same as when I ran into him and he held me to stop me from falling over. It's the real thing. And any moment now, he'll kiss me . . .

Chapter 8 *Christopher comes to stay*

I sit very still waiting for Brad to kiss me. But it doesn't happen. I wait a little longer.

'Brad?' I whisper softly, then I look at him. And I realise he's fallen asleep.

And that, I'm afraid to have to tell you, is as romantic as the evening gets. I sit there until I'm forced to move because my shoulder hurts (Brad's arm is very heavy). When I do move, Brad makes a very unromantic noise through his nose and wakes up.

'What?' he says. 'What's the matter? Oh, was I asleep?' He takes his arm away from my shoulder and yawns. 'Sorry. It's been a really tiring day, don't you think? I'm going to go to bed. The guest bedroom is on the right at the top of the stairs when you're ready. There's a clean towel in the bathroom, and a spare toothbrush. See you in the morning.'

'Good night . . .' I reply as he leaves the room.

I sit there miserably, listening to him go up the stairs, and then finally I take the dirty plates to the kitchen and go upstairs myself. I don't expect to sleep very well. I'm far too unhappy. Nothing I try to do turns out right. Nothing. I'm useless.

Old. Fat. Foolish. Jealous. And now *useless* too.

I sigh, lying there in the darkness, knowing that Brad is asleep in the next room. At least he said I was pretty. He

54

didn't have to say that. And he does look at me in that special way.

Perhaps I just haven't been obvious enough. Perhaps he isn't sure about how I feel. Maybe I just need to simply *tell* him how I feel about him instead of trying to *show* him by cooking meals. Especially if the meal is going to be such a disaster.

Yes, it would be much simpler to just tell Brad how I feel. OK, that's what I'll do. I'll tell him. Tomorrow.

When I wake up next morning, I'm not sure where I am at first. I lie there for a while, looking around me, and then I remember. Hill View House! Brad! Oh no. Today I'm going to tell him how I feel about him!

Suddenly feeling nervous, I lie back against the pillows, trying to imagine it. Perhaps he'll be painting in the studio and I'll walk in behind him and tell him. No, that's not a good idea. He'll get annoyed if he's in the middle of painting. Well then, perhaps we'll go for a walk together if it's stopped raining. Yes, that's a much better idea.

Except that . . . from today I no longer work for Brad! Perhaps he'll be taking me straight back to Brighton! Well, if he does that, I'll just have to tell him in the car. Although if I tell him I'm in love with him as we're driving along, we might have an accident . . .

Suddenly I hear voices downstairs in the hall. Brad is already up, and by the sound of it, he's got a visitor.

'You can't do this to me!' I hear him say. 'I won't be able to manage!'

'Brad, *please*!' The woman speaking to him sounds upset, and I quickly get out of bed and move closer to the door to listen.

'I wouldn't ask you if this wasn't a crisis,' says the woman. 'Don't you see how serious this could be?'

Who is she? Definitely not Tania. Thank goodness.

After a long pause, I hear Brad groan. 'Oh, all right,' he agrees at last, 'but only for three nights, OK?'

Now the woman sounds happy. 'Oh, thank you, Brad!' she says. 'Thank you! Bye, darling, I'll be back for you in a few days. Be good. And don't forget, it will soon be Christmas!'

A door opens and closes, and seconds later I hear a car driving away. Desperate now to know what's happening, I quickly get dressed.

As soon as I'm ready, I leave the bedroom and look down the stairs. There is Brad, standing in the hall. And standing beside him is a little boy.

They both look up at me. I look down at them. For a moment nobody says anything. To be honest, I'm a little shocked. You see, the boy, who looks about six years old, is clearly Brad's son. Even from here I can tell he has the same black hair and dark eyes as Brad. Not only that, but the shape of their faces looks almost the same.

Is Brad divorced?

I go slowly downstairs and as I get nearer I can see the boy looks unhappy. In fact, he looks as if he might be about to cry.

'Hello,' I say, trying to be cheerful. 'I'm Alex. Who are you?'

'Christopher,' he says very quietly.

'He's my sister's son,' Brad tells me, and then he sees my face. 'Alex, you surely didn't think . . . ? Goodness, no!' Brad's voice is filled with horror at the thought of

Christopher being his son. 'No, he's my *nephew*. My sister's marriage is in trouble so she wants to leave the boy with me for a few days. I told her it wasn't a good time, but –'

'Shh!' I say quickly, looking at the boy. 'He can hear you!'

And sure enough, tears are beginning to roll down the little boy's face.

'I'm sorry,' Brad says crossly, 'but it *isn't* a good time. There's this forgery business and the newspapers. I don't even know what I'm going to do about Arthur Grant's cancelled exhibition.'

The gallery, the gallery, the gallery! Sometimes I think that's all Brad thinks about.

'Some things are more important than cancelled exhibitions!' I say firmly, taking the child's cold little hand in mine and leading him towards the kitchen. 'Come on, Christopher, let's make you a cup of hot chocolate.'

'Women!' shouts Brad after me. 'You're all impossible!'

I want to shout something back at him, but I don't because of Christopher. Honestly, how can Brad be so insensitive? I'm really surprised at him. The poor child must be feeling really frightened and alone.

'Daddy shouts too,' Christopher says as I bend down to take his coat off, and his little face is so sad I almost feel like crying myself.

'People get cross sometimes,' I say. 'It makes them say things they don't really mean.' Christopher takes the tissue I offer him, uses it, then hands it back to me. 'That's better,' I say. 'Now, would you like a cup of hot chocolate?'

'Yes, please.'

'Yes, please,' says Brad, appearing through the doorway.

'You can make your own drink,' I tell him, but I can already feel my anger leaving me. He's *looking* at me again.

'Look,' he sighs, 'I'm sorry, OK? I'm sorry, Christopher. You're very welcome here, of course. I've just got a few things I'm worried about at the moment, that's all. I didn't mean to shout.' He smiles at both of us, and Christopher smiles back.

I don't want that smile to work on me. I still feel angry with Brad. Unfortunately I don't seem to be able to do anything about it. When Brad smiles like that I just melt. He has such an attractive smile, you see. It has as much effect as his stare. I can't imagine why some film director hasn't discovered him and made him into a movie star.

'Why don't I make us all a cup of hot chocolate?' he suggests. 'You and Christopher can go into the living room. It's nice and warm in there.'

It's impossible for me to stay angry with Brad for long. I smile back. 'All right,' I say. 'Come on, Christopher.'

The little boy holds my hand. 'Can Uncle Brad make nice hot chocolate?' he asks doubtfully as we leave the kitchen, and I smile.

'I'm not sure, Christopher,' I say, but Brad shouts after us.

'Excuse me, but I make the best hot chocolate in the south of England!'

Christopher and I look at each other and start to laugh, but actually, when it arrives, the hot chocolate is good.

'You see?' Brad says, and I smile at him.

'OK, I agree. You're a hot chocolate expert.'

'Can you cook pizza?' Christopher asks, and Brad frowns.

'Not without a little help from a supermarket. Speaking of which . . .'

'What?'

'Well, for reasons I won't mention, there isn't any food in the house, so someone needs to go shopping.'

'Oh,' I say, but Christopher seems to have stronger opinions about it.

'I don't want to go shopping!' he objects. 'I don't want to go shopping!'

Brad sighs. 'Christopher,' he says, 'please be a good boy.'

'I'll stay here with him while you go to the supermarket if you like,' I offer. 'We can play some games, can't we, Christopher?'

'You do seem good with children,' Brad says as Christopher nods enthusiastically. 'So good, in fact, that I wonder . . .' Brad coughs a little. He seems almost *embarrassed*.

'What?'

'Well,' Brad sighs, 'I agreed to have the boy to stay for three nights. I know I said last night that your job finished from today, but I wonder if you'd work for another couple of days to help me to look after him?'

'Please, Alex! *Please*, Alex! Please!' Christopher is so excited he starts to jump up and down. Unfortunately he's still holding his cup of hot chocolate. Very soon the pale green carpet is decorated with an interesting brown pattern.

Brad covers his face with his hands.

'Sorry, Uncle Brad,' Christopher says very quietly, looking at the mess on the floor.

'You'd better buy something to clean the carpet with while you're in Lewes,' I say.

'Yes,' Brad groans, and then he looks at me. 'Please say you'll stay, Alex,' he says, sounding a lot like his nephew.

For a moment I consider asking Brad why he doesn't ask Tania to look after Christopher. But I have to admit that it does feel good to have him begging me for something. Anyway, I already like the little boy. *And* it will give me more time to tell Brad how I feel about him. As well as two more nights alone with him, after Christopher has gone to bed. There can't be quiz shows on television every night, surely?

So I nod my head. 'OK,' I agree. 'I'll stay.' And this time when Christopher starts to jump up and down I almost expect Brad to join in, he looks so happy.

'Excellent!' He says, standing up. 'I'll go and get that pizza then.'

Five minutes after Brad has left, it starts to rain again. Christopher and I go upstairs to look out of the studio window. Firle Beacon has disappeared once more. The rain is like rain in a jungle.

Poor Brad! I imagine him driving along the narrow country roads through the rain in a bad mood. And I very much doubt whether he's got an umbrella with him.

I notice Christopher is very quiet. 'Are you OK?' I ask him, wondering if he's afraid, or whether he's thinking about his mother and father.

He nods. 'Will there be a storm?' he asks, and I shake my head.

'No, I don't think so. Look. It's already getting brighter. There's some blue sky over there.'

We sit close together, looking out at the view, and suddenly I realise I'm feeling really happy. Brad's right, I am good with children. I understand them. Perhaps it's because I'm always making mistakes and getting into trouble myself!

'Mummy says Auntie Tania isn't very nice,' Christopher says suddenly and instantly I smile. I like this little boy more and more by the minute!

'Does she?'

Christopher nods. 'Auntie Tania told me a story once,' he says. 'It was stupid and boring. Can you tell good stories?'

Can I tell good stories? Of course I can tell good stories! I'm about to write a bestselling book!

'What would you like a story about?'

'You choose.'

'OK then. Give me a minute to think of one.' But it takes me less than a minute. Within seconds I'm telling Christopher a story about a girl and a boy who have very strange parents. Parents who give them *earth* names: Willow and Moon. Yes, I know, it sounds familiar. Well, I've done a lot of *reading* about writing stories, even if I haven't written any yet. The advice is always to start by writing about something you know about. That's all I'm doing. Well, at first, but I make the next bit up. In the story I'm telling Christopher the children *become* their earth names when they go to sleep at night: the girl becomes a willow tree, and the boy becomes the moon.

Anyway, Christopher seems to like it. He's listening with so much attention he doesn't even notice when the blue sky disappears and the skies grow dark again.

Before my story about the children's adventures is finished, a storm has begun and I can hear thunder in the distance.

'I want to have an earth name!' Christopher announces. 'I know, I'll be . . . Forest!'

'That's a nice name.' I smile, and Christopher smiles back at me.

'Your stories are much better than Auntie Tania's,' he says. 'Are you Uncle Brad's girlfriend now?'

Just at that moment, Brad appears at the studio door with very wet hair. He looks at me across the room. My face goes red.

'Oh, hello,' I say. 'We didn't hear you come back.'

'Obviously not,' he says. 'Aren't you going to answer Christopher's question?'

'Yes, of course I am. No, Christopher, I . . . just work for your Uncle Brad. At least, I do for the next two days.'

Christopher (Forest) seems to have no idea at all that he is embarrassing me. 'Well,' he says, 'I wish you *were* his girlfriend, then you could tell me stories all the time!'

Brad laughs. 'Now there's a thought,' he says.

Chapter 9   *Wishes don't always come true*

The thunderstorm soon passes, but it carries on raining all day. By evening we have played all the games we can think of, and watched children's television. Brad has been up in his studio for hours, only coming downstairs to cook and eat pizza. (I'm still not allowed to do anything in the kitchen more complicated than making coffee.)

After I've put Christopher to bed, I try to make myself look nice for the evening, but it's difficult. I've got nothing to change into for a start, and I've just noticed my skirt has patterns of hot chocolate and burnt casserole on it. Clothes aren't the only thing I don't have with me. It's now *ages* since I had a cigarette. I think I'm going to give up smoking by accident!

Anyway, I brush my hair and put on some of the lipstick I've found at the bottom of my handbag. OK, so the lipstick colour is called Sweet Pink, not Terrible Tania Red, but it's the only lipstick I have with me. It will have to do.

I hear Brad finally leave his studio and go downstairs. I take one final look at myself in the mirror. I think I look OK. Of course, I would like to look better than OK, but OK is all I am.

Closing my eyes, I make a wish. Well, actually, I make ten wishes, but they're all about the same subject: what I want to happen tonight.

Here are my wishes:

1. As I walk into the room, Brad will look up at me and smile.
2. He'll pour me a glass of wine and invite me to sit next to him on the sofa.
3. Romantic music will be playing on the stereo.
4. The light from the fire will make me look truly beautiful.
5. Brad will find my conversation interesting and delightful.
6. We'll look into each other's eyes with growing attraction.
7. After a while, he'll pull me into his arms.
8. He *won't* fall asleep.
9. We'll listen to the music like this until, eventually, he pulls me even closer and . . .
10. We kiss.

But none of my wishes will come true unless I actually leave my bedroom and go downstairs!

In the hall, I take a deep breath, and smile with my Sweet Pink lips. Then I open the door and go in. Brad is sitting in an armchair reading a book. He doesn't look up, so he doesn't see either my smile or my lipstick.

I stand in the middle of the room. 'It . . . it's a nice fire, isn't it?' I say nervously, but Brad doesn't look up.

'Well, it's certainly hot.'

The room is very quiet. There's no music playing at all, romantic or otherwise.

'How . . . how did your painting go?'

'Fine, thanks. Is Christopher OK?'

I sit down on the sofa, trying not to feel disappointed that because Brad's in the armchair I can't sit next to him.

Instead, I imagine what it will be like when Brad and I have our own children. Perhaps we'll take it in turns to put them to bed, or maybe we'll do it together, Brad getting them washed, and me telling them a story.

'Alex?' Brad says, 'I asked you if Christopher was OK.'

'Oh! Yes, yes, I think so,' I say. 'A bit worried about his mother and father perhaps –'

'Oh, they'll be all right,' Brad says impatiently. 'They always are.'

I frown. 'Do you mean they argue often?'

'Yes,' he says, 'all the time. I'm getting tired of it, to tell you the truth. My sister always panics and thinks it's the end of their marriage. But it never is – she and her husband always get back together again. Of course, she never thinks I might have problems of my own.' He puts down his book and stares into the fire.

'Are you still worried about the gallery?'

'Yes, of course I am.'

I sigh quietly. None of my wishes are coming true yet. 'You just made a mistake with those paintings, that's all. Nobody's perfect.'

'Hmm,' says Brad. 'The problem is, the public *expects* you to be perfect. Making mistakes is just not professional.'

'I'm sure it will all sort itself out.'

'I don't see how,' he says moodily. 'Sometimes I wish I'd never opened the gallery at all. It's nothing but trouble. Perhaps I need a change of career. The problem is, the only thing I've ever really wanted to be is an artist, and it's very difficult to earn enough money from painting pictures.'

'I want to write a book,' I say after a while and, to my surprise, he laughs.

'You'll never do it!'

I feel really hurt. 'Why do you say that?'

'Because for one thing everybody thinks they could write a book, and hardly anyone does. And for another thing, don't forget I've seen you working at the gallery. You aren't an organised type of person. Writers have to be organised.' He laughs again. 'No, you'll never write a book.'

I'm so disappointed, I just sit there quietly, and eventually Brad realises he's upset me. 'It's nothing personal, Alex. I'm sure you have other strengths.'

But he's just trying to be nice, and, the thing is, I know he's right about me being disorganised. I'm *always* losing things and forgetting things. Not to mention *burning* things.

'Cheer up,' Brad says, and I try to smile. It isn't a very successful smile, but he doesn't see it anyway because he's reading his book again.

'Christopher liked the story I told him today,' I tell him, and he looks up briefly.

'That's hardly the same as writing a book though, is it?'

'Isn't it?'

'No!' Brad sighs. 'Look, can we just leave this conversation?'

'All right.' I sit there feeling miserable while Brad reads his book. The only sound in the room comes from my stomach. The pizza was quite small and we ate it hours ago.

'Do you want something else to eat?' I ask at last, but Brad shakes his head.

'No, not for me, thanks. I've got to go out in a minute.'

I can't believe it. 'You're going out?'

He looks at me. 'Yes. That isn't a problem, is it? You aren't frightened of being here on your own or anything silly like that?'

I can feel my face growing hot again. 'No, of course I'm not! My parents practically live in the countryside. I was born in the countryside. I'm not scared of it at all. I like being close to nature and –'

'Good,' Brad says, getting to his feet. 'I wouldn't go if I didn't have something really important to do in Brighton. Feel free to use the telephone. I won't be back too late. And Alex, thank you for agreeing to look after Christopher. I really am grateful.' He stands in the doorway and gives me a look *and* a smile. Then to finish it off, he pushes his hand through his hair. 'Bye, now,' he says softly.

'Bye . . .'

He allows the smile and the look to last for just a little while longer and then he leaves the room. Seconds later the front door closes after him and I hear his car start up.

And then I'm alone with a small child, in a strange house, in wild stormy weather. And none of my wishes have come true. Not one!

Chapter 10   *Alone without Brad*

I phone my mother quickly to tell her where I am, and then I phone Diana.

'That man's just using you,' she says after I've told her what I'm doing.

'No, he isn't,' I deny crossly. 'He's just . . . worried about things at the moment. If you met him –'

'I know, if I met him I'd understand. I've lost count of how many times you've said that to me.'

'It's true!' I say hotly. Friends can be very annoying sometimes. Especially when they refuse to believe anything you say. 'Anyway, Brad said he had something really important to do in Brighton. He wouldn't have left me all alone here otherwise. I know he wouldn't!'

'He's probably gone round to see Tania while you look after his nephew for him,' Diana suggests cruelly.

'Brad and Tania have broken up!'

'Do you really *know* that, Alex?'

'Well, no, but . . .'

'You saw one argument, that's all. It doesn't mean they've broken up. Look, you won't like me saying this, Alex, but I think you ought to be doing something a bit more useful with your life than chasing after Mr Brad Courtney. Let's face it, you haven't really been happy since you met him, have you? And now he's got himself into this stupid trouble with those fake pictures.'

'How do you know about that?' I ask, amazed.

'It's in tonight's newspaper,' she says. 'There's a picture of you too.'

'Is there?'

'Yes. Actually, you look really guilty about something. It says, "When our reporter asked the unknown woman who she was, she refused to comment."'

'How exciting!'

'Hmm,' says Diana. 'Shall I tell you what I think would be much more exciting? If you wrote down the story you made up for Christopher. If he liked it so much, other children will. You could be a children's writer.'

'No, I couldn't!' I say, surprised. But then I think about the idea. A *children's writer*. It does sound good, I have to admit. 'I wouldn't know where to start!'

'Well, first you get some paper and a pen and then you take the top off the pen and move it over the paper. Easy.'

'Ha ha. Very funny. Anyway, if it's so easy, why haven't you done it?'

'Because I haven't got your imagination. Oh, by the way, Barry phoned me. He wondered if you were at my house as he couldn't reach you at yours.'

'He's only been gone one day!' I complain. 'Does he expect me to wait in every night by the telephone?'

'He hasn't gone anywhere actually,' Diana says. 'His work's been put back for a few days because of the bad weather.'

'Oh. OK. Well, perhaps I'll give him a call.'

But actually, after I say goodbye to Diana, it is quite nice to speak to Barry. I don't have to feel nervous with him. I can just talk.

I tell him everything. Well, *almost* everything. I leave out most of the things about Brad.

'So Diana suggested I should write down the story I told Christopher. You know, make it into a book. What do you think?'

'Fantastic idea!' he says. 'Really fantastic.'

Hmm . . . When I put the phone down, I feel sort of . . . well, confused. It's really nice that Diana and Barry obviously believe I could be a writer. The thing is, Brad definitely doesn't believe it and, at the moment, I'm more likely to agree with him. However, I've got nothing to lose by giving it a try, have I? I'll never know who's right unless I do.

I make myself a jug of coffee and then I find some paper and a pen and sit down to begin. For a while I just chew the end of the pen and drink the coffee. In my mind I can still hear Brad's laughter and disbelief. The thought of him coming home to find me still chewing the end of my pen is what I need to make me begin writing. I'm going to show him he's wrong. By the time he gets back, my story will be finished.

Carefully I write a title at the top of the page. *Earth Children*. Yes! I really like that. And it hardly took me any time to think of it. Perhaps this writing business is going to be easy after all.

Feeling more confident, I start my story. When I reach the bottom of the page, I stop to read what I've written. It's *terrible*. The title is the only good thing. I tear the page up and throw it away. Then I begin again, but unfortunately that attempt is just as bad. I feel just the same as I did at school when I had to take an exam. My mind is filled with ideas, but the words I actually write down aren't the same as the ideas.

After a third attempt I give up and look at the clock. It's almost eleven o'clock. I've used up lots of time writing rubbish. And Brad still isn't home.

Now I'm not writing, I'm conscious of all the noises outside. The weather still sounds wild and the wind is really strong in the trees. I start to worry about Brad. What if he's had an accident? What if a tree's blown down across the road? Or onto his car?

I open the front door and look outside. It is *completely* dark. I've never seen darkness like it. No moon, no stars, no street lamps. Not even any distant street lamps. Certainly no car headlights.

Suddenly something flies right in front of my face. Surprised, I give a little scream.

OK, I know I told Brad I wasn't afraid of the countryside. I'm not really. Well, at least, only a bit. I'm OK if someone else is with me. But nobody is with me, at least nobody except Christopher, and he's only six years old. And you know as well as I do that my parents' house *isn't* in the countryside. Well, not the proper countryside like this, anyway.

Christopher probably isn't used to the countryside either. He could be frightened if he wakes up on his own. Perhaps it would be a good idea to sleep with him. And I'll leave the lights on outside the bedroom door in case he gets up in the night.

When I go into his room, I find him deeply asleep. There's just enough room in the narrow bed for me as well. As I climb in next to him he moves a little, but doesn't wake up. Then I hear him whisper something softly in his sleep, something that sounds like 'Forest'.

I smile, making myself as comfortable as I can in the small space I have. What I'd really like is to just go to sleep now, quickly and easily while I still feel nice being next to Christopher. What I don't want to do is start thinking, because I know that if I start doing too much thinking I'll feel like a failure.

But it's no use, the thoughts are already coming.

I'm frightened of the countryside at night.

I'm hopelessly in love with someone who prefers to spend his time with his horrible girlfriend instead of me. (Because by now even I know that Diana must be right. Brad hasn't had an accident. A tree hasn't blown down. He is with Terrible Tania.)

I haven't bought *any* Christmas presents yet and there are now only six shopping days to go until Christmas.

I'm not going to become a famous children's writer.

And it's not fair!

I lie there for ages, and then just as I'm finally about to fall asleep the telephone rings downstairs. Careful not to wake Christopher, I run down to answer it.

'Hello?'

'Well,' says a familiar voice, 'if it isn't little Miss Mystery Woman!'

Tania!

'Little Miss No Comment!' she continues.

I realise two things at once. (1) Tania is drunk, and (2) Brad can't be with her if she's ringing Hill View House.

'How can I help you, Tania?' I ask politely.

'Well, now,' she says, 'let me see. You could disappear.

72

Yes, that would be good. You could remove your untidy annoying self from Brad's house, Brad's gallery and Brad's life!'

I wait a moment to see if she's finished. She hasn't.

'In fact,' she continues, 'I don't trust you one tiny little bit. Want to know what I think? I think it was you who was responsible for the forgeries. I bet you've got the real Ralph Blackman paintings hidden away somewhere!'

'Now, wait a minute – ' I start to say, but she isn't in the mood to listen to me.

'I want to speak to Brad!' she says. 'Get me Brad now!'

I enjoy telling her the truth. Oh, I really do enjoy it. 'I'm sorry, Tania,' I say sweetly, 'but Brad isn't here. He went into Brighton several hours ago. I'm surprised he hasn't been in touch with you. Must go now. Bye.'

Tania starts to scream something at me, but I put the phone down on her. I feel good for about ten seconds, and then I'm back to feeling worried again.

Where is Brad?

Chapter 11   *Alex Faye – children's writer*

'Alex?'

Suddenly I realise that Christopher is standing next to me.

'Hi!' I say, doing my best to smile, despite feeling worried about Brad. 'What are you doing up?'

'The telephone woke me up.'

'It was your Auntie Tania,' I tell him and he pulls a face.

'Typical!' he says, and I make a guess that he's heard his mother say something similar about his Auntie Tania before. 'Anyway,' he continues, 'she isn't my real auntie. Brad and her aren't married yet. I hope they *don't* get married.'

So do I! Oh, so do I!

'Come on,' I say, 'let's get you back to bed. It's very late.'

'Can I have a drink of milk first?' he asks, and I smile.

'Of course you can. Wait in the sitting-room where it's warm and I'll bring it to you.'

When I go into the sitting-room, he's looking at the only piece of paper I didn't tear up when I was writing my terrible story.

'What's this, Alex?'

I take the paper from him. 'It's the story I was telling you,' I say. 'At least, it was *supposed* to be the story I was telling you. I didn't do it very well.'

'Will you read it to me?' he asks, drinking his milk.

'Oh no, Christopher. It's no good!'

'*Please*!'

I sigh. 'Oh, all right then.' So I read it to him exactly as I've written it on the page.

Afterwards he looks at me. 'That's a different story,' he says.

'No,' I say, frowning, 'it's the same one. Honestly, it is.'

'Well,' he says, 'it's got the same people in it but it sounds funny.'

'Does it?'

Christopher nods, finishing off his milk, and after I've taken him back up to bed I come downstairs and read the story again. And he's *right*. Suddenly I know just what he means. It sounds too *formal*, and it's certainly very different to the way I told it to Christopher. And that makes my story sound cold and distant and even a bit . . . boring.

Oh, thank you, thank you, Christopher! Thank you! I'm so delighted I do a little dance around the room holding the piece of paper. But not for long. I haven't got time. I've got a story to write.

So, I start again, from the beginning. And this time I try to write it down exactly as I told it to Christopher. I'm so involved in it, I don't notice the sounds from outside any more. I don't even think about Brad! Amazing.

By the time I write 'The End' at the bottom of the last sheet of paper, dawn is breaking outside. I feel stiff from sitting for so long, and I stand up and stretch, yawning. You can imagine how tired I feel, yet somehow I don't feel like going to bed. It's too late to go to bed really. Christopher will be up soon.

And Brad still isn't back.

But as I open the front door to look at the sky, suddenly there he is, driving up in his expensive black car.

'Did you wait up for me?' he asks tiredly as he gets out, and I'm about to answer when I notice there's something wrong with his face. His left eye's all bruised and black. He looks as if he's been in a fight!

'What happened?' I ask, running forward and reaching out to touch his face.

'Ow!' he says. 'Careful, it hurts!'

'Sorry. But what happened? Tell me!'

Brad's face is moody. 'Yes, all right, just let me get into the house, would you? I need a drink.'

'I'll get you a drink,' I say, running inside. 'What do you want? A cup of tea?'

'No,' he says, 'I do not want a cup of tea. I want whisky. A very large glass of whisky. And when I've finished that one, I might just have another one. OK?'

'Yes,' I say, 'of course. Why don't you sit down and I'll get it for you?'

'Stop fussing, Alex,' he tells me, but in the sitting-room he sits down in an armchair just as I suggested. When I bring him his drink, his eyes are closed.

'Thanks.' He drinks the whisky in one go and holds the glass out to me. I fill it up again and he drinks half of it, then lies back in the chair, closing his eyes. His face looks very pale next to the dark bruise on his eye, but he's still handsome. If I had a black eye and I drank that much whisky at once I would *not* be looking desirable. Also, I'd be unconscious on the floor, not sitting in a chair.

'Tell me what's happened, Brad,' I say before he can fall asleep, and he sighs and looks at me.

'I've made a complete fool of myself, that's what's happened.'

I look at him, surprised. It just doesn't seem like Brad to admit to feeling foolish. 'How?' I ask.

He drinks some more of the whisky before he continues. 'I went for a drink. You know, that new pub on the seafront. I thought some of my friends would be in there, but they weren't. So I sat and waited in case they came in later, and suddenly I saw *him*.'

'Him?'

'Yes, *him*, the monster who sold me those fake Ralph Blackmans.'

'Goodness!' I say, staring at him. 'So you went over and hit him?'

Brad doesn't answer for a while, just looks down into his glass at what's left of his whisky. 'Not exactly, no. I . . . well, I sat and looked at him.'

'You *looked* at him?'

'Please stop repeating everything I say, Alex. It's very annoying.'

'Sorry. I'm just trying to understand, that's all. And at the moment, I don't understand. How did you get a black eye from looking at someone?'

'He noticed me looking,' Brad says at last, but he says it so quietly I can't hear him.

'What?'

'I said he noticed me looking!' he shouts. 'He saw me looking and he came over and asked me why I was staring at him. He said, "I don't like the way you're staring at me," and then . . . well, then he hit me.'

'Just for looking at him?'

'Yes! The next thing I know the police are there, but *he's* gone – left with his friends. And I have to spend the rest of the night at the police station looking at photographs to try to identify him.'

'How exciting!' I say without thinking and Brad frowns at me.

'Alex, sitting in a cold police station with a black eye in the middle of the night looking at photographs of ugly people is *not* exciting, believe me. You should try it some time.'

'No,' I say, 'I don't suppose it is. Sorry. Anyway, did you find his photograph?'

'No, I did not. I've got to go back later to look at another five hundred photographs. If you think it's so exciting, perhaps you'd like to come with me!'

Of course, I don't have to tell you I definitely *would* like to go with him, but actually, in the end, things don't turn out like that. Because at that moment Christopher comes downstairs in his nightclothes. Brad takes one look at him and seems to become even more tired than ever.

'I'm going to bed,' he says, and off he goes.

Christopher seems fed up. 'Uncle Brad doesn't like me,' he says.

'Of course he does, Christopher!' I tell him, but he shakes his head.

'No, he doesn't. He wouldn't even look at me!'

I remember Brad's black eye. 'Ah, well, I think that's because he's hurt his face a bit. I don't think he wanted you to see it.'

Christopher's eyes light up with interest. 'Really? Is he all covered in blood?' he asks. 'Does he look really horrible?'

Boys! 'No, of course not. He'll be better soon. He just needs to rest now.' I need to rest too after my night of story writing, but obviously I'm not going to get the chance.

Christopher's looking miserable again. 'It's boring here,' he says. 'It doesn't even feel like it's nearly Christmas!'

He's right. It doesn't feel as if it's nearly Christmas.

'OK then,' I say, 'let's *make* it feel like Christmas. Let's buy a Christmas tree and make some decorations for it.'

'*Yes!*' Christopher is happy once more, running straight upstairs to get dressed, and within half an hour we're walking up the lane in the direction of the farm shop.

Christopher's running on ahead, singing to himself, something that sounds like a carol, a Christmas song, and suddenly I feel happy. I also feel *strange*, because I'm so tired. It's almost as if my feet aren't quite touching the ground. But I do feel happy. Diana was right. I do feel better now I've started to write. If *Earth Children* still seems all right when I read it again, I'll type it up on Dad's computer and post it off to a publisher. I'm a *writer*!

Suddenly I see a car coming towards us. 'Careful, Christopher!' I warn him. 'Move to the side of the road.'

'OK, Alex,' he says happily, doing as I asked straight away. I'm smiling at him, thinking what a good boy he is, when suddenly I recognise the car coming down the lane towards us. It's *Barry's* car.

'What are you doing here, Barry?' I ask him when he stops. He lifts his eyebrows, pretending to feel hurt.

'That's not a very nice way to welcome me when I've taken a day off work specially to see you.' He smiles, and I can feel my face going red. Which is amazing, actually, because in all the time I've known Barry, I don't think I can remember that happening to me before. Mind you, I'm not sure he's ever looked at me in quite the way he's looking at me now. Anyone would think we'd been away from each other for weeks, not for just thirty hours or so.

'I didn't mean it like that,' I say. 'It's good to see you. Of course it is. I was just . . . surprised, that's all.'

'I wanted to surprise you.' He smiles at me, and then Christopher joins us, so Barry smiles at Christopher too. 'Now you must be Christopher,' he says.

'Who are you?' asks Christopher.

'I'm Barry, Alex's boyfriend,' Barry says confidently. Well, why wouldn't he be confident about it? I haven't told him he *isn't* my boyfriend yet.

'Good!' Christopher says. 'I didn't really want Uncle Brad to be her boyfriend. We're going to buy a Christmas tree. You can come with us and put it in your car!'

Chapter 12 *The two Bs (Barry and Brad)*

Barry looks at me. My face is red again. 'A Christmas tree,' he says thoughtfully, 'that's exciting. Of course we can put it in my car.' And he opens the car door for us without asking anything at all about 'Uncle Brad'.

Still, somehow it's a happy thing to do, buying the tree. Christopher's so excited that we end up feeling excited too, and there's Christmas music playing in the shop and coloured lights and decorations. As well as the Christmas tree, we buy a very large cake and a bottle of wine. I'm not sure I'll have any of the wine because I'm so tired. I already feel a bit drunk and unsteady on my feet. But I *definitely* want some of the cake. Mmm . . . delicious.

I only start worrying about Barry and Brad meeting each other when we're driving back towards the house. Still, hopefully Brad will still be asleep.

I open the front door very very quietly.

'Uncle Brad!' shouts Christopher at the top of his voice. 'Uncle Brad, come and look at the Christmas tree!'

'Christopher!' I whisper loudly. 'Be quiet! Shh!' I can feel Barry looking at me. 'Brad . . . that is . . . your Uncle Brad was awake all night. He's very tired.'

'But it's daytime now,' says Christopher, 'and I want him to see the tree!'

Barry's still looking at me. 'You seem very tired yourself, Alex,' he says. 'Very tired.' Suddenly I realise what he's thinking. He thinks Brad and I are both tired because we were awake all night making love to each other!

'I was writing,' I tell him quickly, 'the story I was telling you about. I wrote it down. I didn't finish until a few hours ago.'

Barry smiles. 'That's great,' he says. 'I'd love to read it later. Now, Christopher, where do you want this tree?'

As I stand and watch the two of them set the tree up in the big entrance hall I start to yawn. Barry looks at me. 'Why don't you have a sleep?' he says. 'We'll be all right for an hour or so, won't we, Christopher?'

'Of course,' says his new young friend, and I smile gratefully.

'OK, I think I will.' Upstairs lying on my bed, I start to wonder why I wanted to make it clear to Barry that nothing had happened between me and Brad, but before I can come up with an answer, I've fallen asleep.

I'm asleep for ages. When I finally wake it's almost lunchtime. Oh dear. I'd better find out how Barry and Christopher are getting on. I'm about halfway down the stairs when I hear a woman laughing. It seems to be coming from the kitchen. I freeze on the middle step, listening.

Surely it isn't Tania? The unknown woman laughs again. No, I doubt if Tania *ever* laughs like that, except perhaps at her own jokes. Then I hear Barry laughing too. Whoever the unknown visitor is, she's certainly got a sense of humour. Perhaps it's Christopher's mother come to collect him. Perhaps she's managed to make it up with her husband, so now she's feeling happy.

I hurry on down the stairs, and then suddenly I see the

tree and stop again, gasping with delight. It looks *beautiful*, with pretty lights, proper decorations and even a star on top!

'Isn't it great?' says Christopher, coming out of the sitting-room, and seeing me. 'Barry had all the decorations in his car! He was going to put them on his tree at home, but he said I could have them instead!'

I stand there looking at the tree, and for some reason I feel like crying. For the first time it really does seem as if it's almost Christmas. 'It's lovely.'

'And your friend's here!' Christopher announces. 'Come and see!'

I follow him into the kitchen, and there, sitting at the kitchen table drinking coffee with Barry, is Diana.

'Di!'

'Hi, Alex!' She smiles at me. 'I was doing a delivery this way, so I thought I'd pop in for a visit. I'm owed some time off anyway. Barry tells me you've written your story. That's fantastic! Well done!'

'Well,' I say, 'it still needs some work.'

'Of course, but the important thing is you've made a start.'

Barry pours me a coffee and I sit down with them at the table. I feel a little confused, to be honest. I mean, for Barry and Di to be laughing together like that, I suppose Di must like Barry. I'm not sure they've been alone together before. They've met, of course, but always as part of a group, and Barry can be a bit shy in a large group.

'And was I right?' she asks me. 'Do you feel good now?'

'Yes,' I say. 'Exhausted, but good.'

Barry's smiling at me, and I remember the Christmas

tree. 'Thanks for being so nice to Christopher. The tree looks really – '

But I don't manage to finish my sentence, because suddenly somebody starts shouting out in the hall. When we leave our coffee and run out to see what's wrong, we find Brad at the bottom of the stairs, staring at the Christmas tree.

'What the hell's that thing doing here?'

We all stand there looking at him, but before we can answer, a car pulls up outside. 'Bloody hell!' swears Brad. 'What now?' And he goes to open the door.

'Goodness me!' says a very familiar voice. 'You *must* be Brad! May I say what a wonderful place your house is in. That view is *beautiful*. And what a delightful Christmas tree!' My mother walks, uninvited, into the hall as her taxi drives off. 'You see, Alex,' she says, 'unlike you, some people are as enthusiastic about Christmas as I am.'

Brad watches as Mum takes off her green coat. She's wearing her short yellow dress. He turns to me, 'Alex,' he asks, 'who is this person?'

I open my mouth to reply, but Mum gets in first. She steps forward to shake his hand, and as she does so, we all notice her shoes at the same time. The left shoe is green, and the right shoe is yellow.

'How silly of me,' she says. 'I'm Alex's mother, Willow.'

Christopher breaks the silence that follows this announcement. 'Is that your earth name?' he asks. 'Mine's Forest!'

I don't think I'll ever really understand how it happens, but somehow, within half an hour, Mum has found Brad some pills for his headache and successfully persuaded him we should have a 'before Christmas' party.

'Your mother's amazing,' Barry tells me, as Christopher leads him upstairs to show him something in his bedroom. 'Really amazing.'

I try to smile, but I can't quite manage it. Mum's got Brad blowing up balloons in the sitting-room, and I can hear her telling him all about me as a little girl. Incredibly *embarrassing* things about me as a little girl. Brad seems *really* interested. He's staring at my mother with complete attention. Either that or his face has frozen with shock. I can't quite be sure.

'Are you OK, Alex?' Diana asks as she passes on her way to the kitchen.

'No,' I say, 'I'm having a bad dream. A *very* bad dream.'

She laughs. 'It's not so bad,' she says. 'Come and help me sort out some party food.'

I'm not sure how she does it, but somehow Diana manages to create a tray of delicious snacks. Not only that, but she also makes me feel as if I am a fairly useful helper, *and* nothing gets burnt.

When we take the food into the sitting-room, Brad is impressed.

'Mmm,' he says to Di, helping himself from the tray, 'I'm really hungry. You're a very clever woman.' And he stands there eating and staring at Di. He only notices I'm there at all when I drop the biscuit I'm eating on the floor.

'Why is it you never learnt to cook like that yourself, Alex?' he says. 'Is it because you were too busy pushing toys up your nose?' Still laughing, he goes over to Di to get another snack. I sit down miserably in one of the armchairs. 'Look,' I hear Brad saying to Di, 'I'm sorry I reacted like that about the Christmas tree. I wouldn't want you to get the idea I was mean. That's not what I'd like you to think of me at all!'

Mum's noticed the way Brad's standing close to Di, looking into her eyes. Or at least, the way he's *trying* to look into Di's eyes, because Di's just carrying on putting the snacks onto plates from the tray as if she doesn't know he's there.

'I thought Brad was going to be *your* boyfriend,' Mum says to me while the others aren't listening. 'Why's he looking at Diana like that?'

'Perhaps,' I say tiredly, 'he isn't attracted to people who used to push their toys up their nose.'

'But, darling,' she objects, 'that was *sweet*! Even the man at the hospital thought so! I was just trying to give Brad a complete picture of you.'

'Hmm,' I say. 'Actually, I don't think your embarrassing stories about my childhood have got anything to do with it. I think he just looks at all women like that – as if he wants to *eat* them.'

You see, suddenly I know it's true. I thought that way he had of staring into my eyes was special to *me*. But now he's doing just the same thing to Di. He was even doing it to my mother! It's just something he does automatically whenever he looks at a woman. I expect he even looks at June Weatherby like that!

Chapter 13 _Coloured white_

Mum squeezes my shoulder. 'Never mind, dear,' she says. 'Anyway, I don't think Diana's interested in him, do you?'

Over the sound of the music we hear Brad asking Diana if she wants to look at his paintings.

'No thank you,' she says. 'I'm not really interested in art. I prefer stories. I'm looking forward to reading Alex's story. She's a children's writer, did you know?'

Good old Di!

My mother goes over to them. 'I'd like to see your paintings, Brad,' she says. 'Very much indeed.'

But Brad doesn't look very happy with this idea. 'Oh, would you, Mrs . . . er, Willow?' he says. 'Well, do please go and look. The studio's at the top of the stairs on the left.'

And off Mum goes, looking a little annoyed that Brad doesn't want to show his pictures to her himself.

A loud song is playing on the stereo, and I can't hear what Brad and Di are saying any longer. I'm just about to get up and go for a walk, or do _anything_ that takes me away from Brad, when Barry comes in.

'Has the party got going yet?' he asks, sitting on the arm of my chair.

'It has for some people,' I say, looking at Di and Brad.

Barry looks at them too. Then he looks at me. 'Your mum's keeping Christopher happy upstairs,' he says. 'Do you feel like going for a short walk with me?'

But at that moment Diana breaks away from Brad. 'Come on, you two,' she says. 'This is supposed to be a party! Let's have some dancing!'

I must tell you I've never felt *less* like dancing in all my life. Yet somehow, there I am, with the rest of them, moving my body to the music. Brad doesn't look as if he wants to dance either. Actually, he isn't very good at it. It's quite surprising actually, the way he looks so . . . well, *unnatural* is as good a way of describing it as any. He doesn't seem to have a sense of rhythm at all. Whereas Barry's always been a really good dancer, much better than I am.

'Do you mind if I borrow Barry for a *salsa*?' Diana asks me when a South American song starts playing, and I shake my head.

'Of course not.'

Brad and I stand and watch. If you've ever seen a couple *salsa* dancing, you'll know how close the man and woman's bodies get to each other. They touch almost all the time. In fact, sometimes *salsa* dancing can look a lot like . . . *making love*.

'I'm not sure you should have agreed to that,' Brad tells me. 'I think your friend's trying to steal your boyfriend.'

'Of course she isn't!' I say, but suddenly, watching Di and Barry together, I feel really . . . well, *strange*. And somehow I can't help remembering how they were laughing together in the kitchen earlier on.

'Perhaps we should make them jealous,' Brad suggests, and next thing I know, he's taken me into his arms and he's bending his head and . . . *he's kissing me*!

After that, everything happens at once. Barry and Diana

stop dancing. Somebody rings on the doorbell. I push Brad away from me so hard he almost falls over. Mum comes into the room. (She appears to be wearing some sort of strange paper hat. It looks as if it might be made from one of Brad's drawings from the studio.)

Then Christopher rushes in. He's holding something. A picture. 'Look!' he says. 'I've painted a picture of the Christmas tree!'

The doorbell rings again, but the sound is drowned by Brad's cry. 'My painting!' he screams. 'My white painting! Christopher! What have you done?'

'Oh,' says my mother. 'I gave him that to paint on. Sorry, did I do something wrong? It didn't look as if there was anything on it.'

There is a long silence, broken only by the ringing of the doorbell. Then suddenly I hear someone laughing. I don't realise at first that it's *me*.

'I'm sorry. Oh, I'm so sorry, Brad,' I say, but it's no good, I can't help it. You see, the white picture looks so much better with a little bit of colour on it. Bright *Christmassy* colour.

Brad looks at me as if he hates me. 'Alex,' he says, 'as of this moment you are no longer an employee of the Courtney Art Gallery. I suggest you leave at once. And you can take your family and friends with you!'

And suddenly everyone's laughing. *Everyone*: me, Barry, Di, Mum and even Christopher. In fact the only person not laughing is Brad.

'Come on,' says Barry through his laughter, 'I think we'd better go.'

The doorbell's still ringing. When we open the door, we

find three people waiting outside: a man, a woman, and
. . . Tania.

'Mummy!' shouts Christopher. 'Daddy!' And the man
pushes past Tania to pick up his son and lift him high into
the air.

'Hello, son!' he says. 'Wow, look at that Christmas tree!
It's *almost* as big as the one we've got at home waiting for
you to decorate!'

When Christopher comes back down to earth we all
crowd round him in a big happy group. Somehow Tania
manages to push her way past us.

'Brad,' she says, 'who are all these *horrible* people?'

We all leave soon after that. Christopher goes home with
his parents, Diana gives my mother a lift back to
Rottingdean, and I . . . well, I go with Barry.

At first we're rather quiet with each other. I think we
both feel a little shy. Either that, or we both know that
whatever we say to each other in the next hour or so is
really important.

Finally, Barry looks at me. 'Do you feel like going for a
walk?' he asks, and I nod.

'Yes, I'd like that.'

'We could go up Firle Beacon, if you're wearing the right
shoes for it?'

We both look down at my *unsuitable* shoes. 'These are
fine,' I say.

'There might be mud,' Barry says doubtfully.

'It's OK,' I say. The fact is, I just want to be with Barry.
In rain, in mud. Anywhere. I know you might find that
difficult to believe after all I've said about him, but it's
true.

You see, when I saw Barry and Di dancing like that, it did feel really strange. Oh, I know it was only a dance to them, but it did make me think. For the first time I thought about what it would be like if I *didn't* see Barry any more. What it would be like if he got a new girlfriend. It wasn't a pleasant thought at all. And suddenly I knew why I'd never managed to tell Barry it was over between us. I hadn't really *wanted* it to be over.

'For a moment there, I thought you were attracted to Brad,' Barry says as we walk along a path through the mud.

'No!' I say, taking his hand, and, strange as it sounds, it isn't a lie. Honestly!

I *know* I've wanted Brad to kiss me for weeks. I *know* I said I wanted to marry him and have his babies. But the fact is, when he kissed me . . . *nothing happened*. I didn't feel anything. Not one thing.

Diana was right. I had a *crush* on Brad. I was attracted to him because of his good looks, and I thought that meant I was in love with him. But the truth is, I didn't know him at all. These last few days I've had the chance to get to know him much better, and . . . well, I now realise I've never seen him properly. In my mind, I made Brad into the type of person I wanted him to be. But that Brad never really existed.

Brad's never been interested in me. He's not even very interested in his nephew. Brad is only interested in Brad. In fact, he's really rather shallow.

'Oh, Alex,' Barry says suddenly, 'look at your legs!'

I look down at myself. I'm *covered* in mud. It isn't only on my legs, but all over my clothes too. 'It doesn't matter,' I say.

Barry laughs, putting his arm around me. 'No,' he says, 'it doesn't, does it?'

Chapter 14   *Happy Christmas*

Well, it's Christmas Day. I'm at my parents' house (as usual). We've just eaten a huge Christmas dinner: roast turkey, carrots and potatoes (as usual). We've sung some Christmas carols together (also as usual).

The one very *unusual* thing is that Barry's here with us. He's sitting between Mum and me on the sofa. He arrived about ten o'clock this morning with a huge bag of presents, and spent the morning helping Mum with the dinner. I could tell Mum was a bit doubtful at first. But that was because she's used to my Dad and my brother being so hopeless in the kitchen. Barry's actually quite good.

Anyway, me and Dad could hear Mum and Barry chatting away in the kitchen as they worked, so maybe she doesn't think he's boring any more. Besides, I think she's missing my brother a little this year. He's fallen in love with a girl in Scotland called Sky, so he isn't with us this year. Sky! Remember I told you he lives on the Isle of Skye? *Very* appropriate.

Any moment now we'll start opening our Christmas presents, but before that, let me tell you what's been happening over the past few days (apart from me rushing about doing my last-minute Christmas shopping).

I read in the newspaper that the man who gave Brad that black eye has been arrested, so presumably Brad returned to the police station to look at some more photographs. I *don't* know if Tania went with him, but I *do* know that she and Brad are engaged to be married. In the circumstances, because Tania is (a) difficult (b) unpleasant and (c) impossible to please, I *don't* think I can say that Brad's story has a happy ending.

As for Christopher's story, his parents were so grateful to me for looking after him they sent Di round with some Kiss Flowers (my third bunch in less than a week!).

And me? Well, Barry took me to a *salsa* dance the other night. I couldn't do the dance properly, but it was very nice to be held as closely as that. We're going to go to lessons together in the New Year.

Also, you'll be very glad to know that as well as the shopping and the *salsa* dancing, I have found the time to read through my story again. *And* I still like it. Straight after Christmas I'm going to start typing it up.

'Time for presents!' Mum says now. 'Here you are, Barry dear. A very Happy Christmas to you!'

'Thank you, Willow!' he says and opens the package she hands to him. Inside is the brightest shirt that has ever been made anywhere in the world, ever. No chance of anyone accusing Barry of being boring in that!

I give Barry a painting – a painting of a bridge. Well, he does like bridges!

'Did you get this from the Courtney Art Gallery?' he asks me, smiling.

'No! Definitely not.' I laugh. Brad would *hate* this painting. It looks like a bridge, you see.

'Well, I think it's beautiful,' Barry says. 'Thank you, Alex. Thank you very much.'

Then it's time for me to open my present from him. Whatever it is, it's in an excitingly large box. Carefully I open it and put my hand inside. I touch something that feels like . . . a shoe.

'Ski boots,' Barry tells me, smiling. 'I thought you could use some to go with this.' He hands me an envelope. Inside there are two plane tickets to Austria.

'I thought you might like to go on a skiing holiday,' he says, and then I'm screaming and kissing him both at the same time.

By the way, that's another thing I've changed my mind about. Barry can be as nice to me as he wants to be!

Later on me and Barry leave my Mum and Dad playing a game of cards and go for a walk along the seafront in the dark together. 'Barry,' I say to him, 'when my *fortieth* birthday comes round, do you mind if we just stay in together and watch television?'

He looks surprised. 'No, of course not.'

'No balloons? No songs?'

He laughs. 'Was it that terrible?'

I nod.

'Sorry. I just wanted you to be in no doubt about how crazy I am about you. But I promise. When you're forty we can do whatever you like.'

When I look up at Barry, he bends to kiss me.

I'm kissing him back enthusiastically when suddenly I hear a crashing sound behind me.

'Look out!' Barry warns me, but too late. Sea water falls from the sky and lands on both our heads.

'We forgot to play the running from the waves game!' I cry, rubbing the water from my eyes, and Barry grabs my hand.

'Well, let's play it now then!' he says, just as another

wave bangs against the wall and shoots up into the air.

'Yeeess!' I scream, and we run madly along in the darkness, racing the wave. And after that one, we do it with the next one. And the next.

And yes, I'm very wet and very cold, and yes, it's a crazy kind of thing to do on Christmas Day. I'm certain my parents have done it many times. Oh, and *of course* I'm not wearing the right shoes for such an activity.

You didn't really think I would be, did you?